1ST GRADE PHONICS
Unit 3
Phonograms 27–49

MW01593561

TABLE OF CONTENTS

IMPORTANT: Please refer to the Teacher Guide for specific scripts, procedures, and words that are represented by pictures.

Throughout this Unit, learners will scan QR codes. Be careful they scan each code individually.

LEARN

- Multi-letter phonograms
- Vowel team and r-controlled syllables
- VCCV and VCV syllable division

VOCABULARY

consonant digraph

vowel team

r-controlled vowel

vowel team syllable

r-controlled syllable

DAILY PAGE GOALS

Day	Complete	Day	Complete	Day	Complete
1	ii–5	7	33–34	13	65–66
2	6–10	8	35–42	14	67–72
3	11–15	9	43–48	15	73–79
4	16–18	10	49–51	16	80–86
5	19–26	11	52–58	17	87–92
6	27–32	12	59–64	18	93–94

1. WHAT DO **sh**, **th**, AND **ch** SAY?

Learn:

- Write and say the sounds for digraphs **sh**, **ch**, and **th**.
- Read questions and exclamations.

Vocabulary:

consonant digraph [ˈkŏn sǐ nǐnt ˈdī grǎf] – two letters that make a consonant sound

**Listen and review.
Mark ☒ when done.**

PHONOGRAMS

In this Unit, you will learn more multi-letter phonograms. We underline multi-letter phonograms. This helps us remember the letters work together.

Phonogram **qu** is a multi-letter phonogram.

Match the words with the pictures.
Underline **qu** and read the words.

1) quiz

2) quilt

3) Quin

3

A **consonant digraph** has two letters. The letters work together to make a consonant sound.

shell   bru**sh**

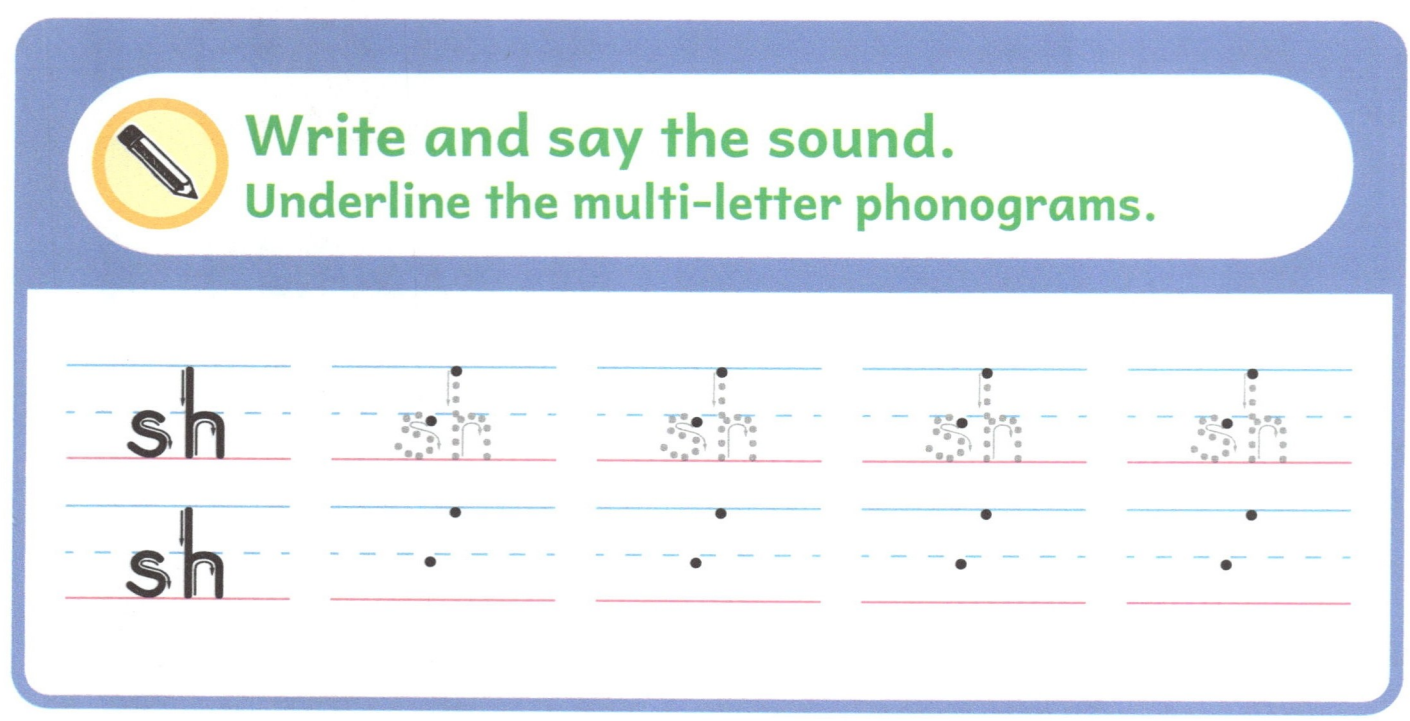

✏️ **Write and say the sound.**
Underline the multi-letter phonograms.

sh

sh

throw   that

Digraph **th** is voiced at the beginning of many everyday words. The rest of the time, it is usually unvoiced.

Write and say the sounds.
Underline the multi-letter phonograms.

chimp chemist mustache

Digraph **ch** makes its first sound most of the time.

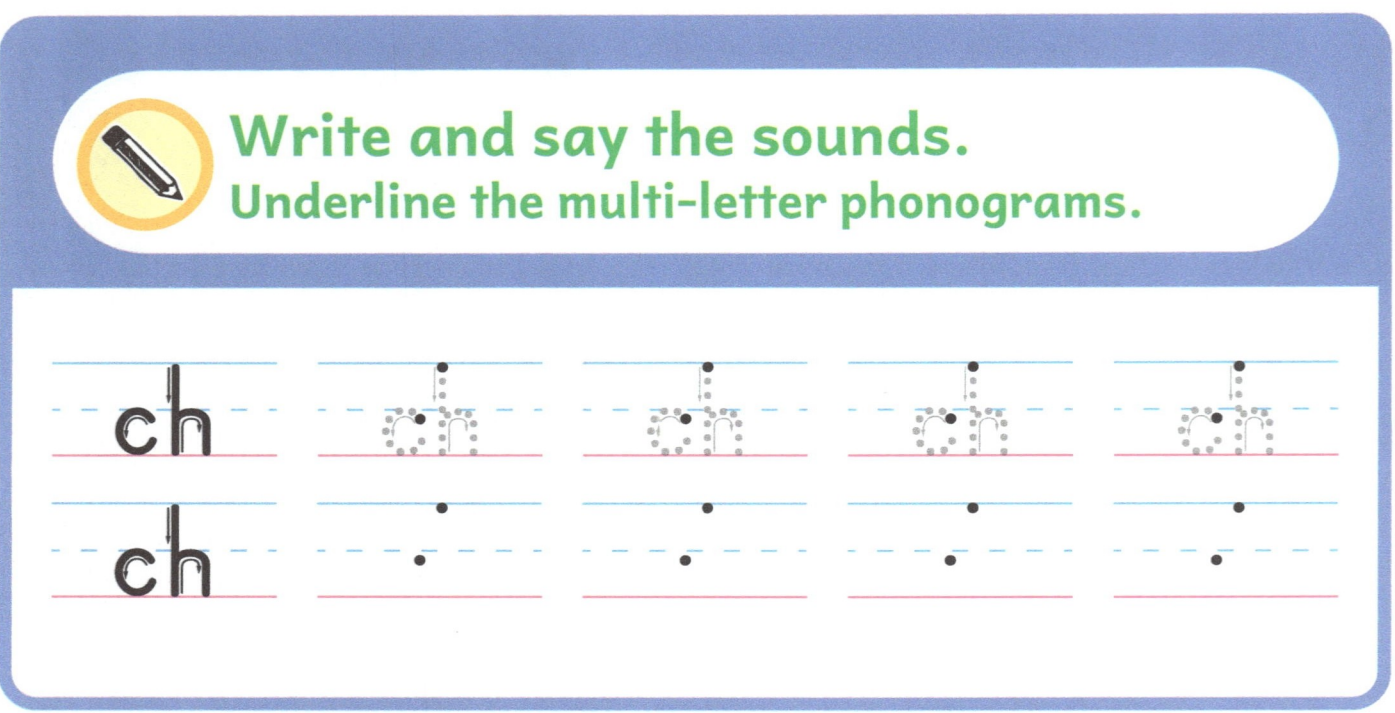

Write and say the sounds.
Underline the multi-letter phonograms.

6

 **Read and write the words.**

| cash | she | ship |

4)
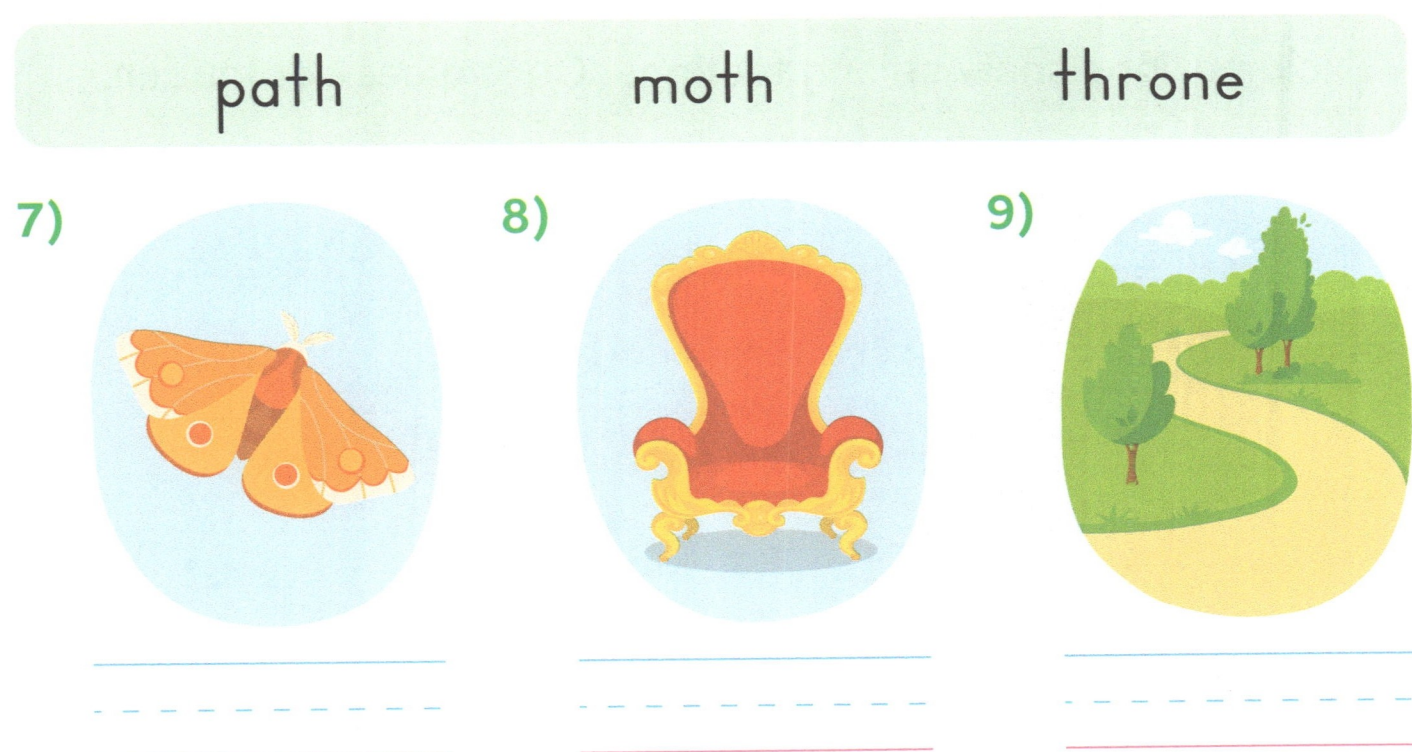

5)

6)

| path | moth | throne |

7)

8)

9)

| lunch | chase | chin |

10)

11)

12)

WORKING WITH WORDS

Questions and exclamations are sentences. Questions ask something. Our voices go up at the end.

Exclamations show strong feelings. Our voices get louder.

Questions

Can pigs fly?

Exclamations

I hope so!

13) Can the bus stop? She left a doll!

14) Is that a crab? It is on my bed!

15) Did Chad and I win? Yes!

WRITING PHONOGRAM REVIEW

✏️ **Listen to and write the phonograms.**
Underline any multi-letter phonograms.

SCORE ○ **CORRECT** ○ **RESCORE** ○

Learn:

- Write and say the sounds for multi-letter phonograms **er** and **ee**.

- Read vowel team and r-controlled syllables.

Vocabulary:

r-controlled vowel *[r-kŭn ´trōld ´vow ŭl]* – a vowel that makes a different sound because it is followed by the letter **r**

r-controlled syllable *[r-kŭn ´trōld ´sĭ lŭ bŭl]* – a syllable with an r-controlled vowel

vowel team *[´vow ŭl tēm]* – a vowel teamed up with other letters to make a vowel sound

vowel team syllable *[´vow ŭl tēm ´sĭ lŭ bŭl]* – a syllable that has a vowel team

Listen and review.
Mark ☒ when done.

WORKING WITH SOUNDS

READING PHONOGRAM REVIEW

R-controlled vowels have a vowel followed by the letter **r**. The letter **r** changes the vowel sound.

h**er** j**er**sey

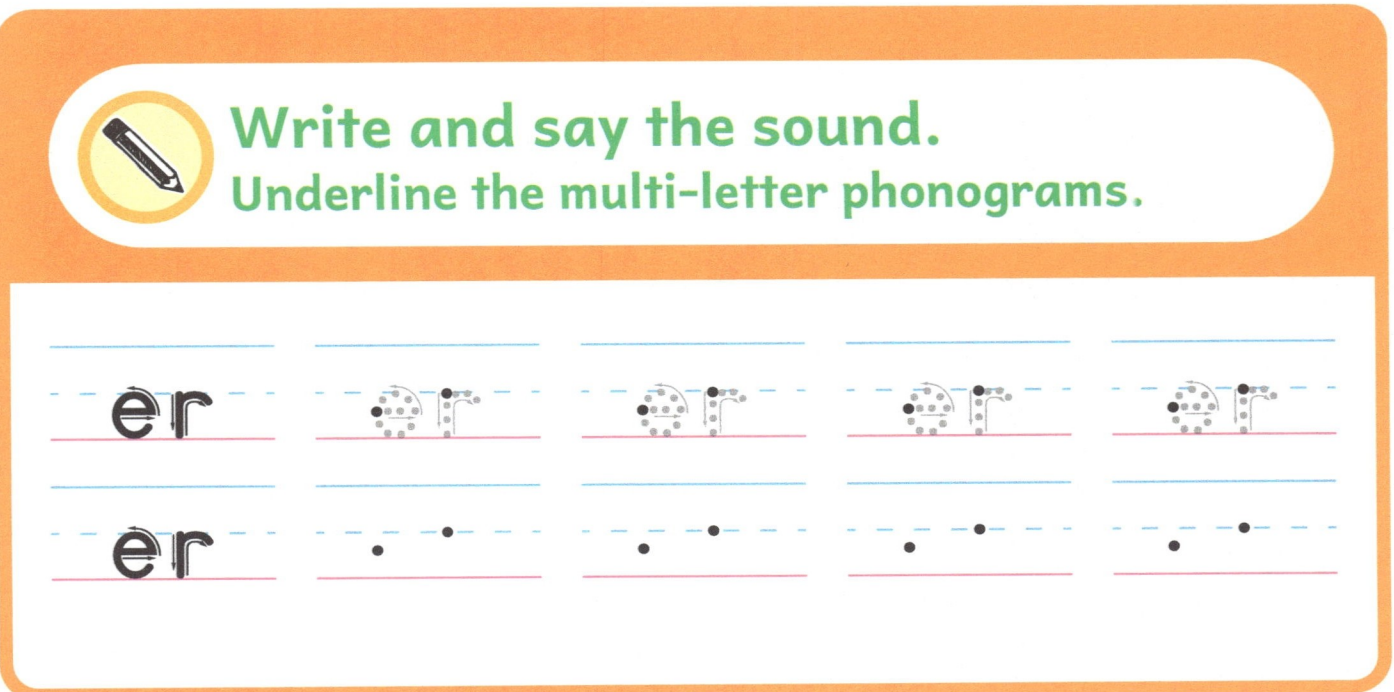

Write and say the sound.
Underline the multi-letter phonograms.

er   er   er   er   er

er   •   •   •   •

Vowel teams have two or more letters. The letters "team up" to make a vowel sound.

eel   sn**ee**ze

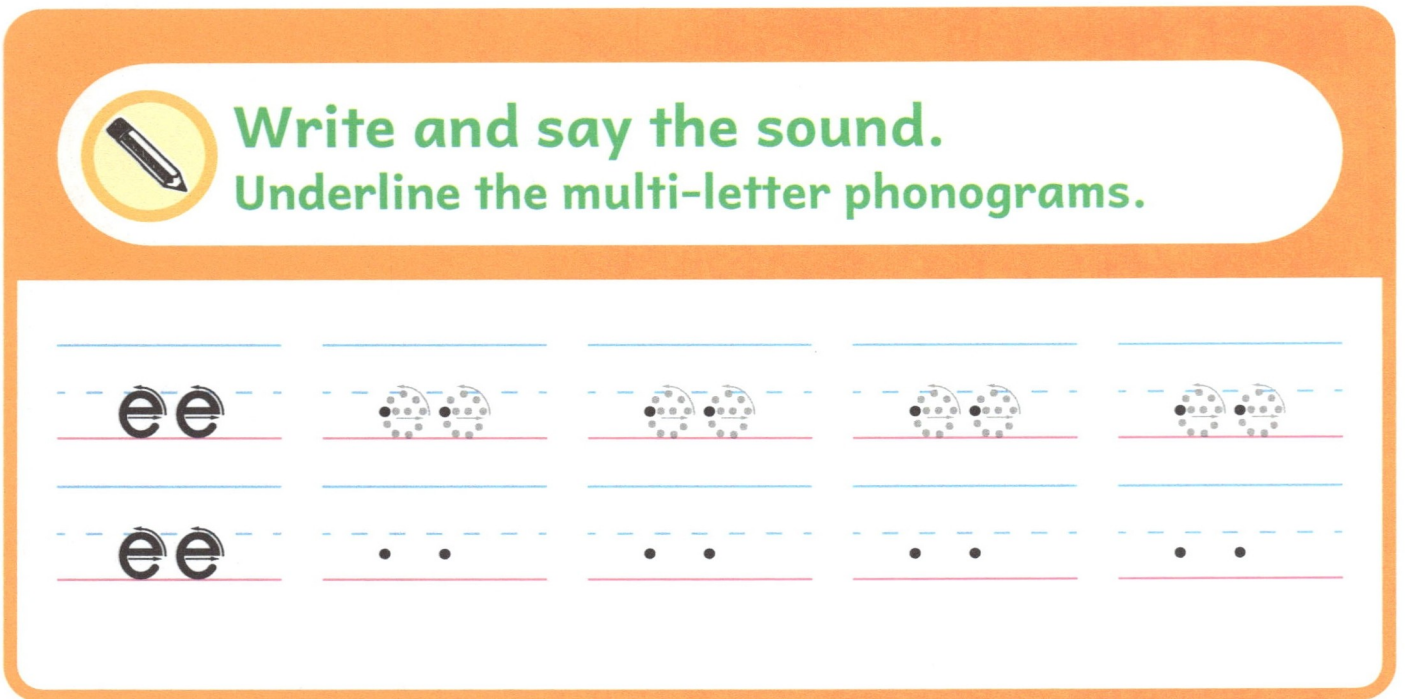

Write and say the sound.
Underline the multi-letter phonograms.

ee ee

ee ee

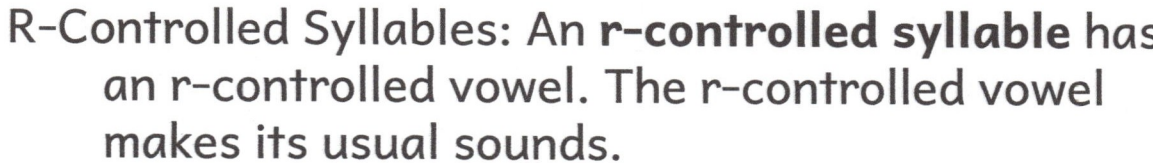

Reading Rules

R–Controlled Syllables: An **r-controlled syllable** has an r-controlled vowel. The r-controlled vowel makes its usual sounds.

Vowel Team Syllables: A **vowel team syllable** has a vowel team. The vowel team makes its usual sounds.

h**er**d   sh**ee**p

 # Read and write the words.

| her | seed | bee | verb |

1)

go

- - - - - - - - - -

----

2)

- - - - - - - - - -

----

3)

- - - - - - - - - -

----

4)

- - - - - - - - - -

16

✏️ **Listen to and write the phonograms.**
Underline any multi-letter phonograms.

SCORE CORRECT RESCORE

ACTIVITY: Reading Rules

Underline all multi-letter phonograms. Count the number of sounds. Circle the syllable type.

	Word	Number of Sounds	Closed	Open	Vowel Team	R-Controlled
1)	<u>sh</u>op	2 ③ 4	Ⓒ	O	VT	RC
2)	green	2 3 4	C	O	VT	RC
3)	per	2 3 4	C	O	VT	RC
4)	the	2 3 4	C	O	VT	RC
5)	term	2 3 4	C	O	VT	RC
6)	cheek	2 3 4	C	O	VT	RC

3. WHAT DO oo, oy, AND oi SAY?

Learn:

- Write and say the sounds for vowel teams **oo**, **oy**, and **oi**.
- Read words with vowel teams.

Listen and review.
Mark ☒ when done.

WORKING WITH SOUNDS

READING PHONOGRAM REVIEW

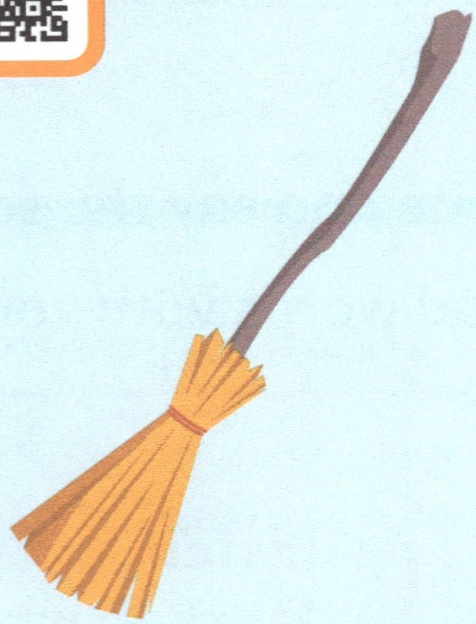

w**oo**d   br**oo**m

Write and say the sounds.
Underline the multi-letter phonograms.

OO

OO

r**oy**al   **oy**ster

✏️ **Write and say the sound.**
Underline the multi-letter phonograms.

oy   oy   oy   oy   oy
oy

m**oi**st   s**oi**l

Write and say the sound.
Underline the multi-letter phonograms.

oi   oi   oi   oi   oi

oi   ..   ..

 # Read and write the words.

toy	boy	joy

1)

2)

3)

coin	oil	point

4)

5)

6)

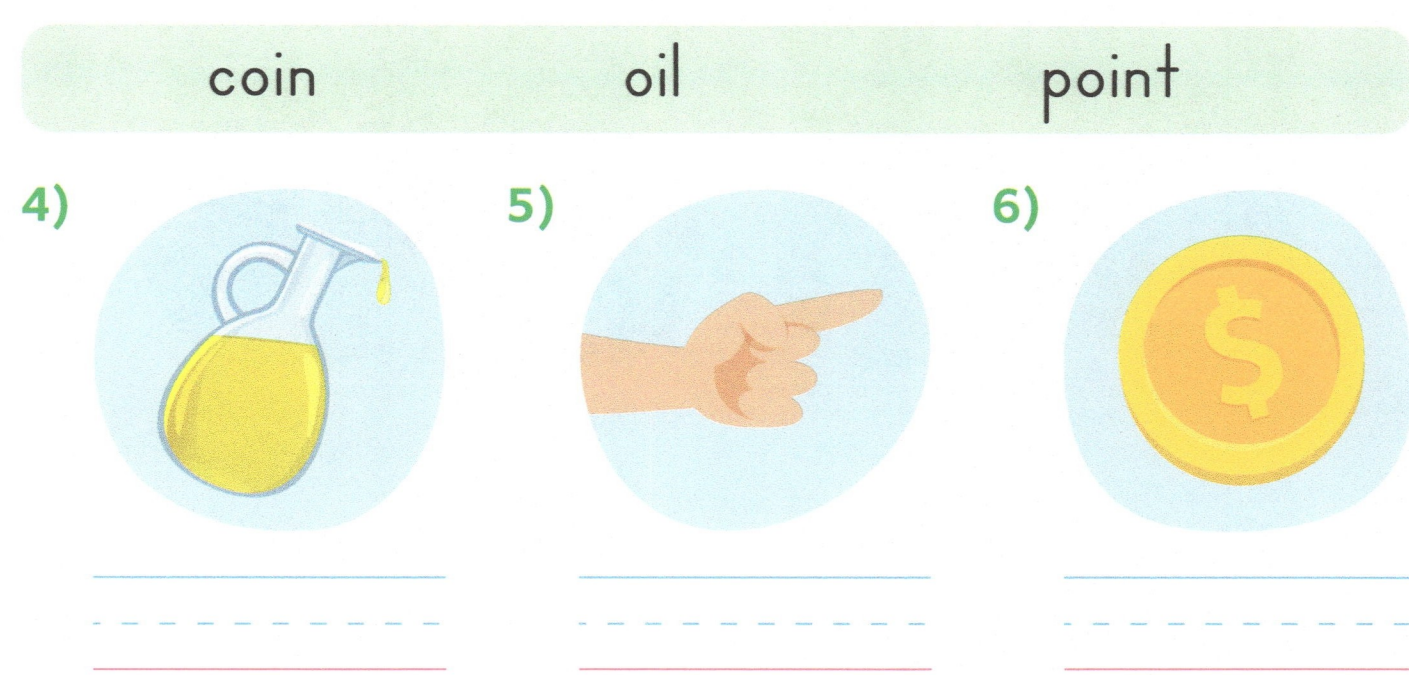

Reading Rules

1st Sound of **oo**: Most of the time, we only use the first sound of vowel team **oo** before the letters **k**, **d**, or **t**.

2nd Sound of **oo**: Vowel team **oo** can make its second sound any time. It can be in any position. It can be before any letter.

cook wood   zoo food

 **Read and write the words.**

book   foot   pool   moon

7)

8)

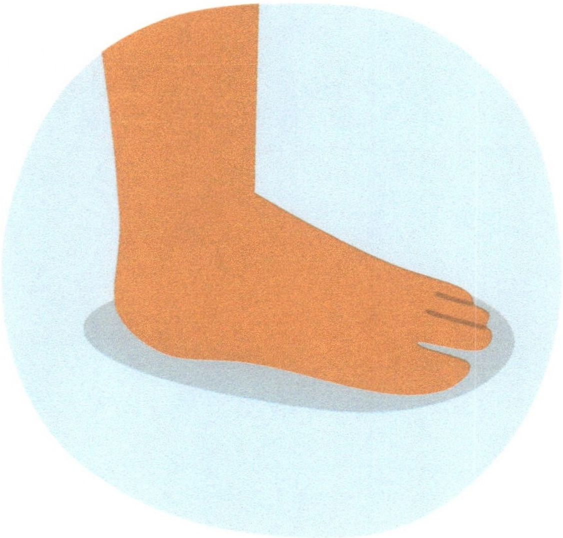

9)

10)

WRITING PHONOGRAM REVIEW

Listen to and write the phonograms.
Underline any multi-letter phonograms.

SCORE · CORRECT · RESCORE

PHONOGRAM REVIEW

? Listen to and circle the correct phonograms.

1)   l   g   b

2)   th   ch   sh

3)   s   sh   t

4)   ee   oo   oi

5)   i   oi   a

6) p　　j　　g

7) ch　　th　　t

8) i　　ee　　e

9) er　　oo　　oy

10) h　　sh　　th

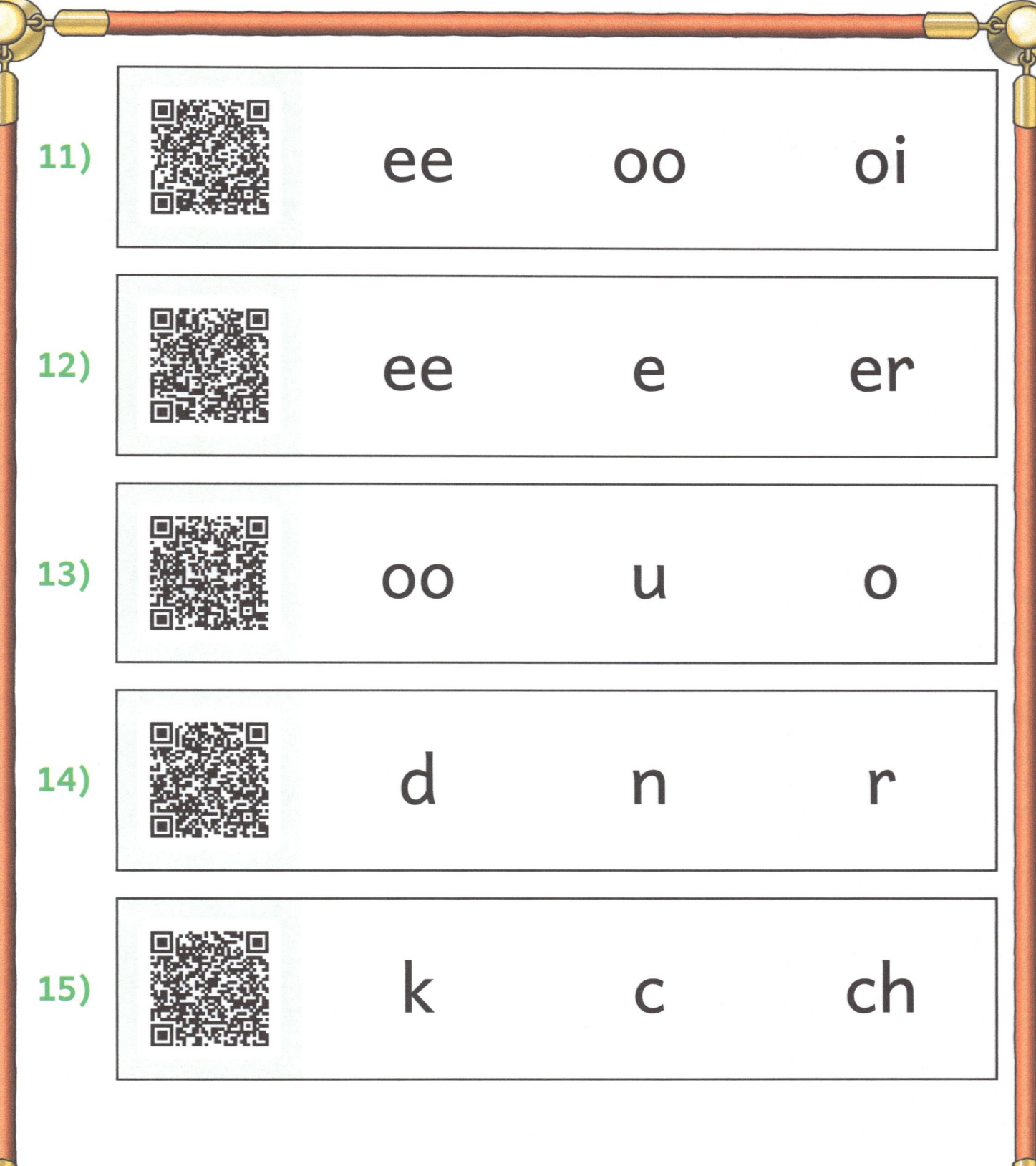

11)   ee   oo   oi

12)   ee   e   er

13)   oo   u   o

14)   d   n   r

15)   k   c   ch

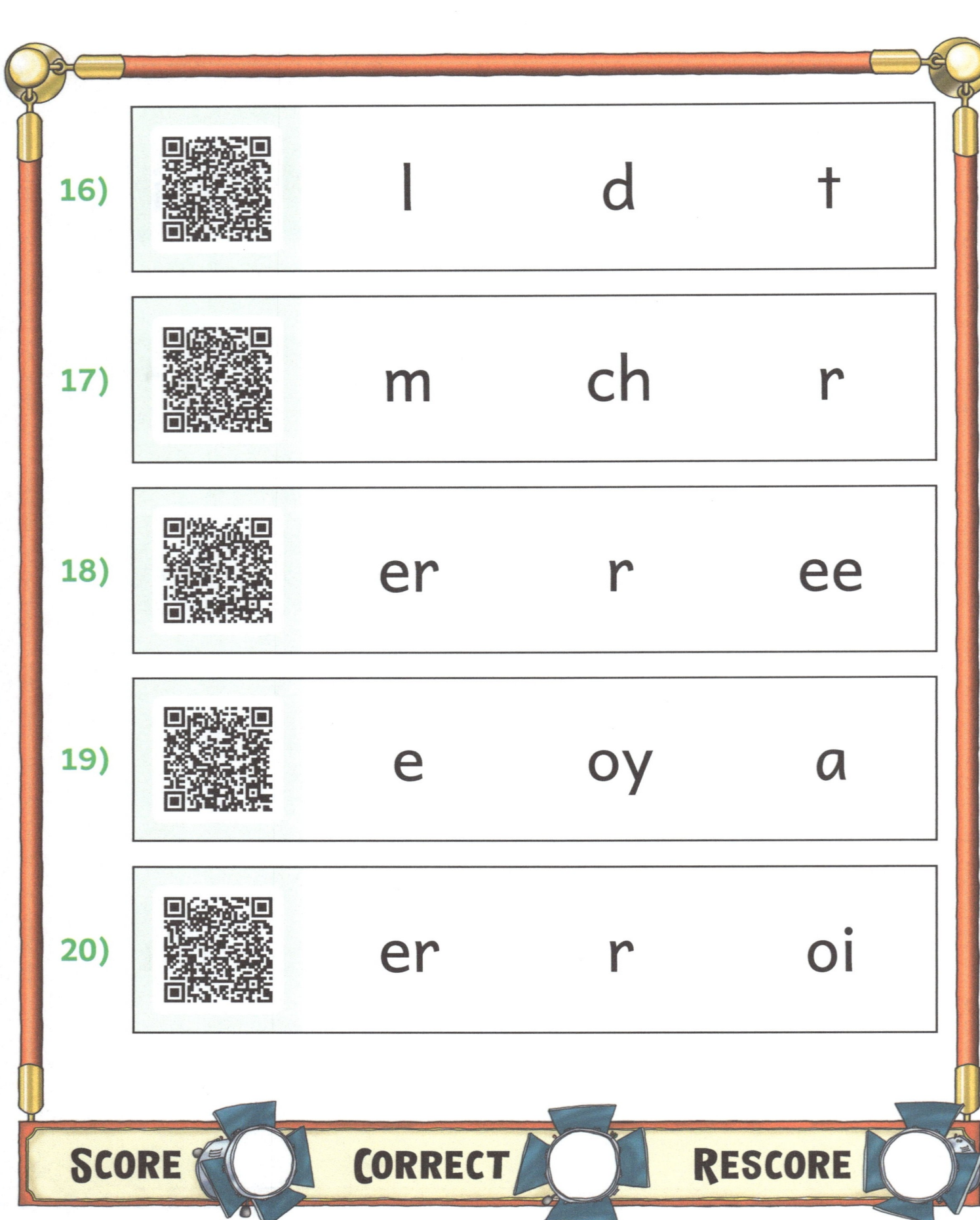

16)   l   d   t

17)   m   ch   r

18)   er   r   ee

19)   e   oy   a

20)   er   r   oi

SCORE   CORRECT   RESCORE

READER 2: "Fun in the Reef"

Practice these everyday words.

Read	Trace	Write
1) the	the	
2) and	and	
3) her	her	
4) see	see	
5) look	look	
6) with	with	
7) good	good	
8) these	these	

? **Choose the correct answers.**

9) What did the characters do first?
   ○ find toys
   ○ eat lunch
   ○ dive into the water

10) Where did the characters find toys?
    ○ in a chest
    ○ on the sand
    ○ in a shop

11) Who made lunch?
    ○ Pip
    ○ Kit
    ○ Bix

Phonogram Test 7

Listen to and write the correct phonograms.
Underline the multi-letter phonograms.

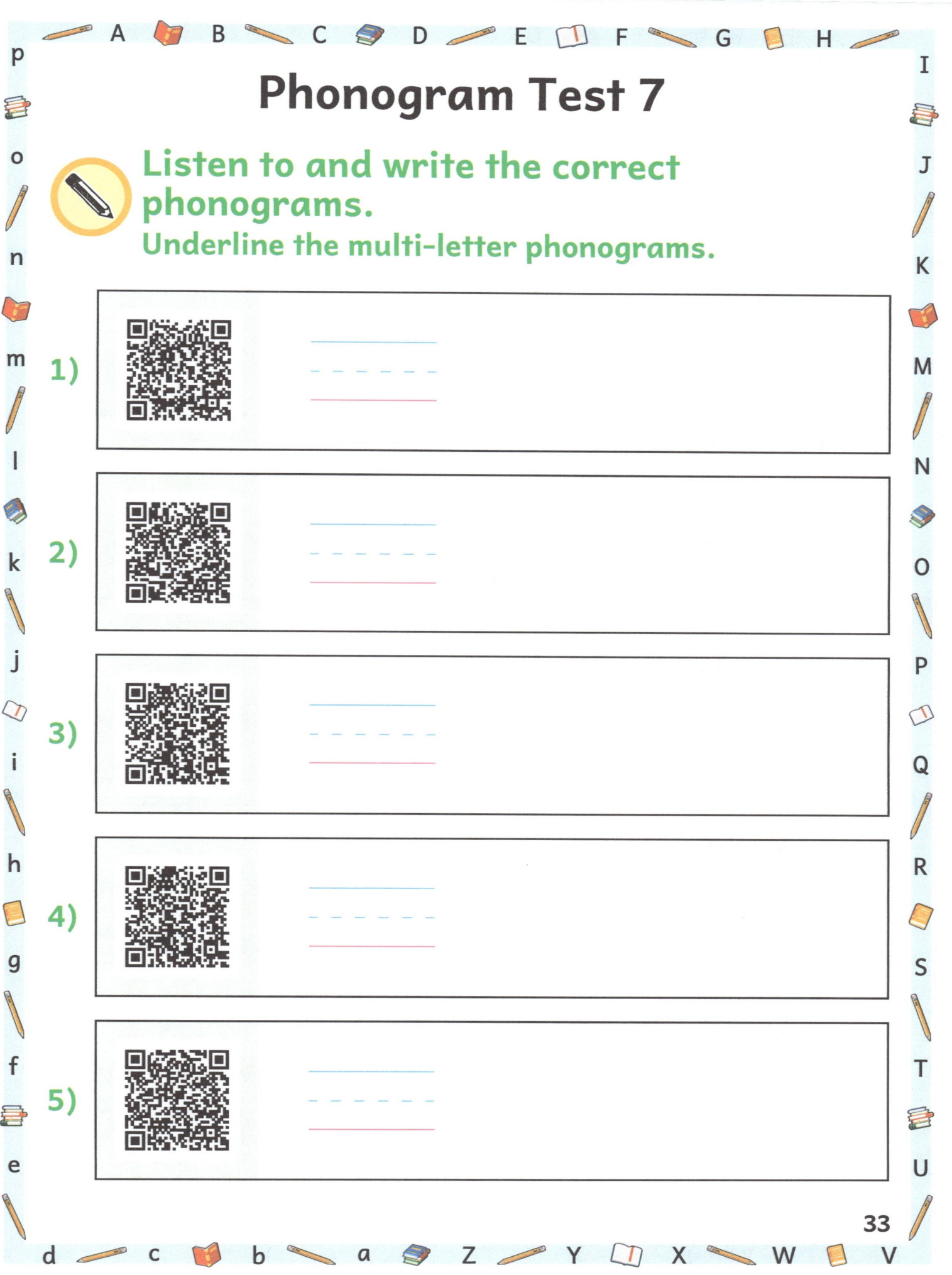

1)

2)

3)

4)

5)

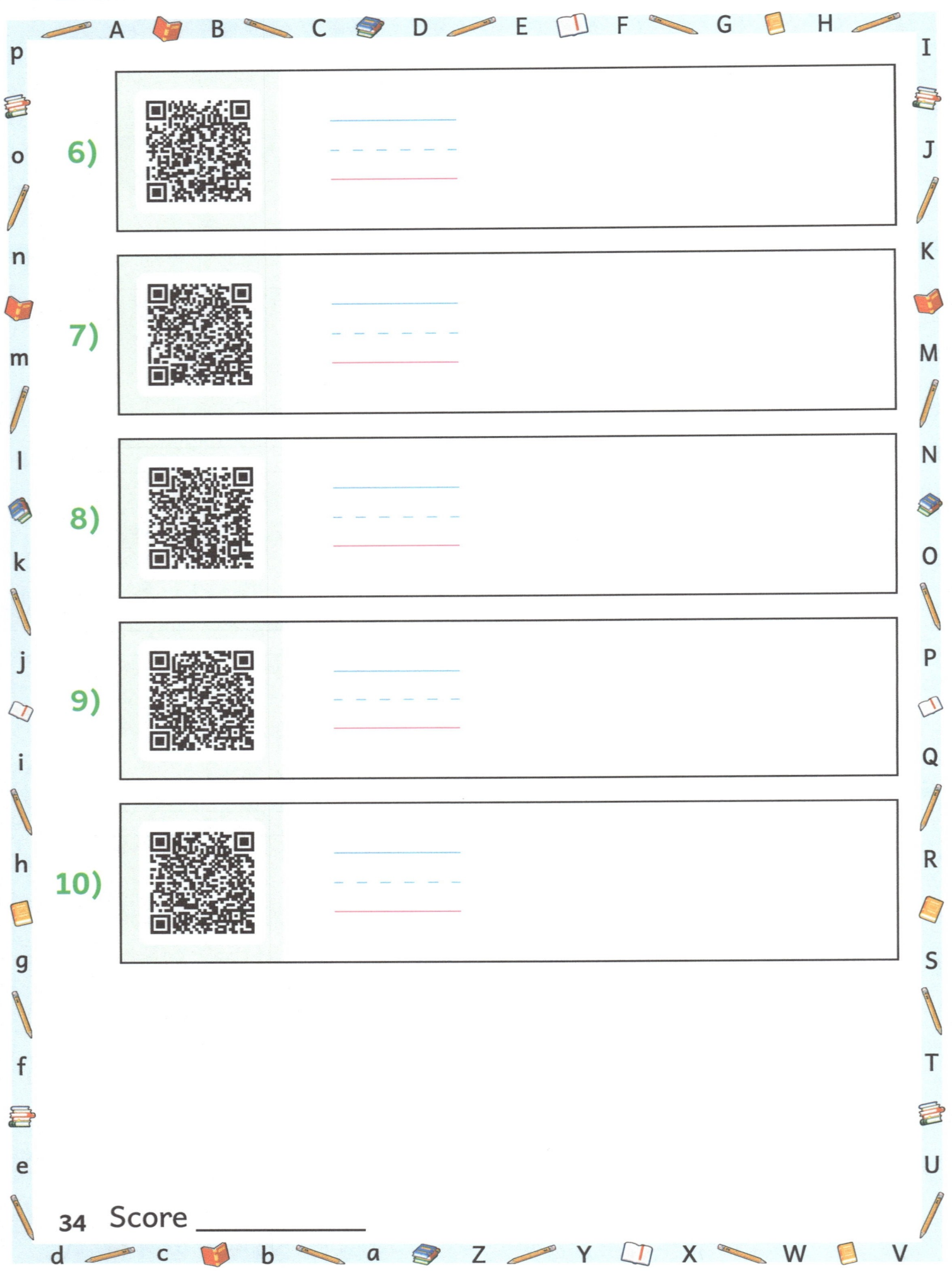

Score _____

4. WHAT DO **ow** AND **ou** SAY?

Learn:

- Write and say the sounds for vowel teams **ow** and **ou**.
- Divide and read two-syllable words.

Listen and review.
Mark ☒ when done.

br**ow**n b**ow**l

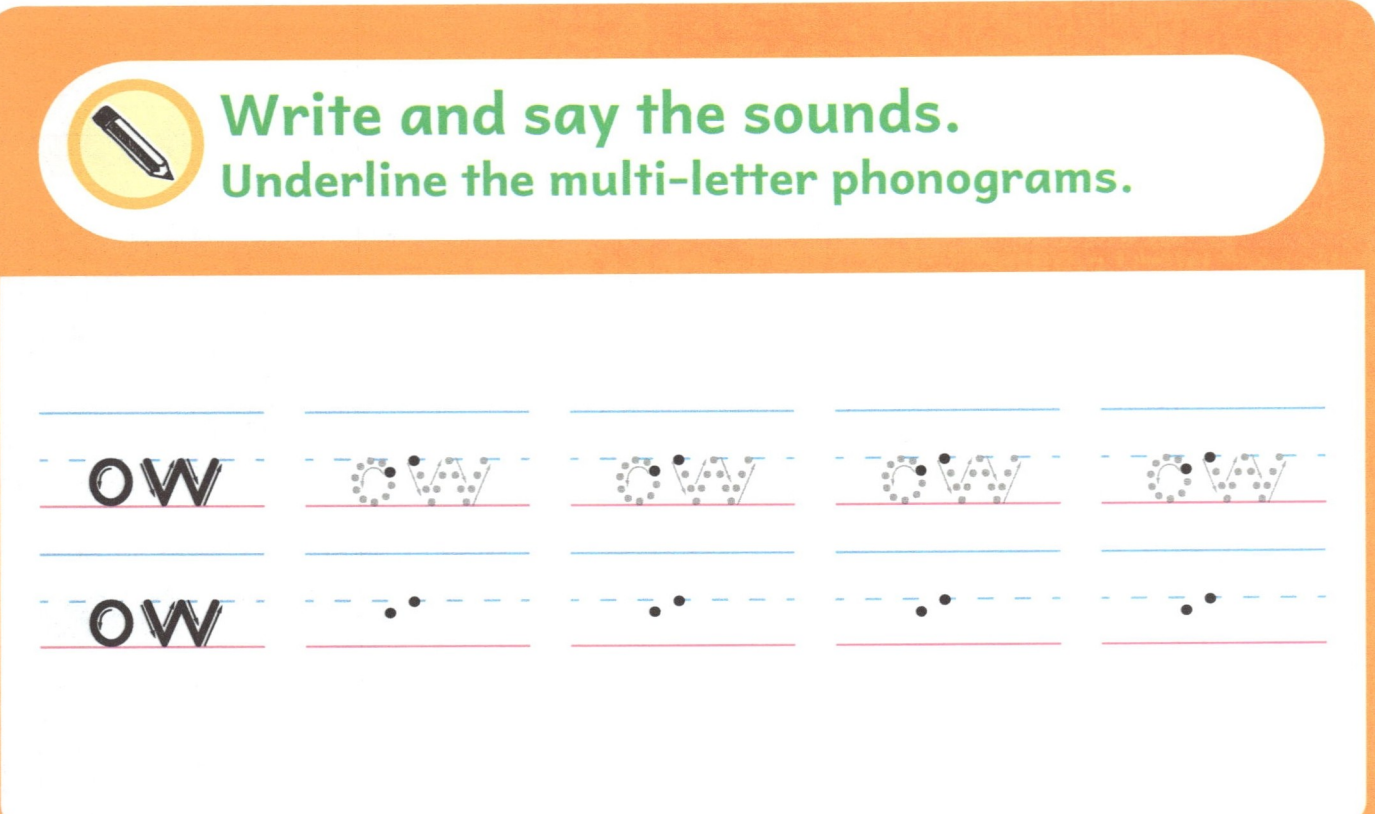

Write and say the sounds.
Underline the multi-letter phonograms.

ow

ow

36

ou

fl**ou**r p**ou**ltry
c**ou**pon marvel**ou**s

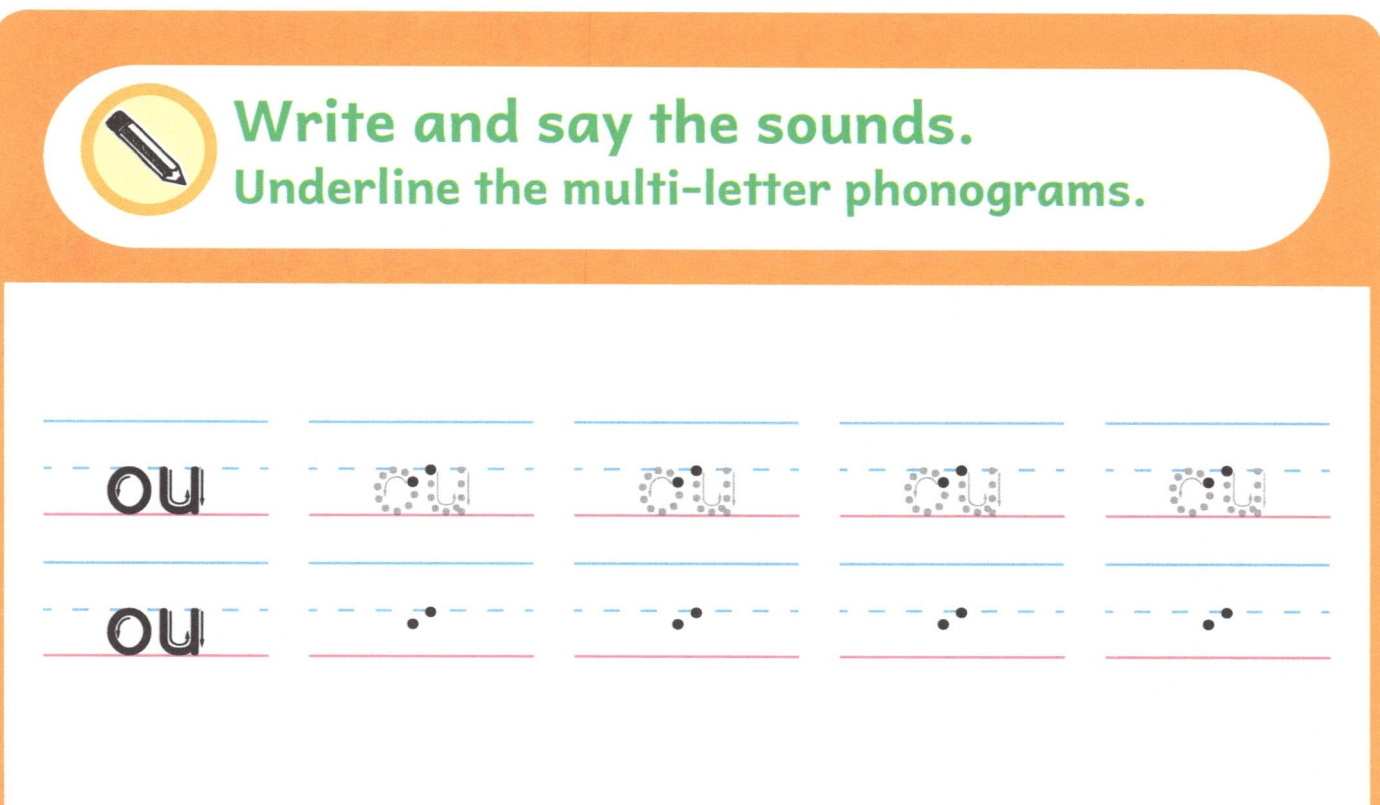

Write and say the sounds.
Underline the multi-letter phonograms.

ou ou ou ou ou

ou

Vowel teams **ow** and **ou** can be tricky. They have similar sounds.

 **Read and write the words.**
First sounds of **ow** and **ou**

cow	cloud	out

1)

2)

3)

 **Read and write the words.**
Second sound of **ow**

blow	row	grow

4)

5)

6)

38

Read and write the words.
Third sound of ou

you	soup	wound

7)

8)

9)

Match the phonograms with the pictures.

10) | OU

11) | OW

WORKING WITH WORDS

You will begin reading words with two syllables. Syllable division patterns will help you. Syllable division patterns tell us how to divide words.

Find a Pattern

1 – Mark the vowels with a V.

2 – Mark the consonants between the vowels with a C.

3 – Identify the pattern.

These words have a VCCV pattern.

VCCV Words: Divide VCCV words between the two consonants.

v c | c v
a n | v i l

v c | c v
t e m | p o

Now, identify the syllable types and read.

v c | c v
a n | v i l
closed   closed

v c | c v
t e m | p o
closed   open

 **Mark, divide, and read the VCCV words.**

v c | c v
candid   pastel   pronto   disco

banjo   jumbo   fabric   submit

✎ **Listen to and write the phonograms.**
Underline any multi-letter phonograms.

SCORE CORRECT RESCORE

5. WHAT DO **ay**, **ai**, AND **ck** SAY?

Learn:

- Write and say the sounds for multi-letter phonograms **ay**, **ai**, and **ck**.

- Divide and read two-syllable words.

(((**Listen and review.
Mark ☒ when done.**

st**ay**   aw**ay**

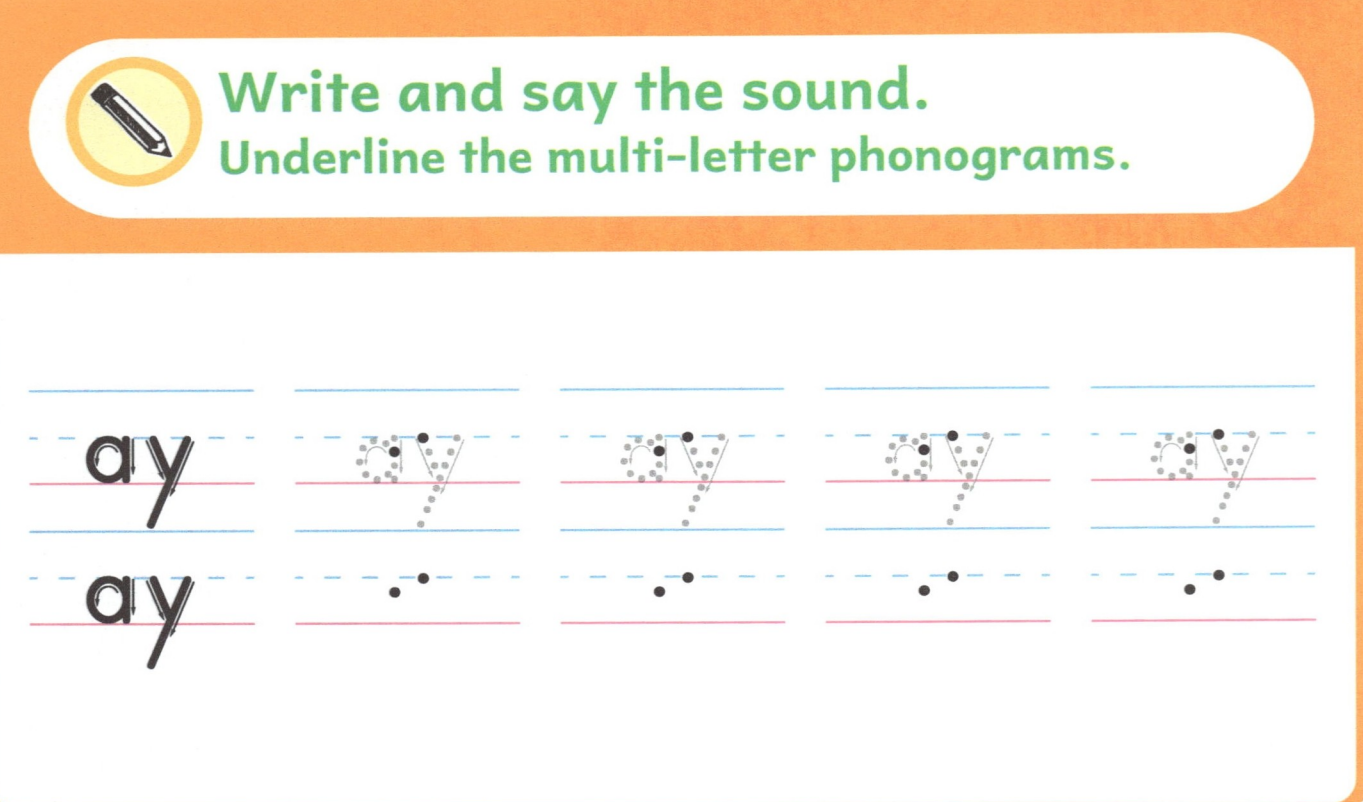

Write and say the sound.
Underline the multi-letter phonograms.

ay   ay   ay   ay   ay
ay

br**ai**d   h**air**

✏️ **Write and say the sound.**
Underline the multi-letter phonograms.

ai   ai   ai   ai   ai

ai

du**ck**   qua**ck**

ck   ck   ck   ck   ck

ck   ·   ·   ·   ·

 **Read and write the words.**

| say | day | clay |

1)

2)
3)

| stain | aim | rain |

4)

5)
6)

block	sock	truck

7)

8)

9)

WORKING WITH WORDS

The VCCV pattern helps us see when the first syllable is closed. Many VCCV words have double consonants. The second consonant is usually silent. Its job is to give the word the VCCV pattern and keep the first syllable closed.

v c | c v
f o s | s i l

v c | c v
h i p | p o

 **Mark, divide, and read the VCCV words.**

happen

Ellen

lasso

hello

tennis

muffin

traffic

motto

Griffin

attic

rabbit

mitten

WRITING PHONOGRAM REVIEW

Listen to and write the phonograms.
Underline any multi-letter phonograms.

ACTIVITY: Everyday Words

Read, trace, and write the words.

Read	Trace	Write
play	play	
day	day	
say	say	
back	back	
how	how	
down	down	
found	found	
out	out	
you	you	
show	show	

6. WHAT DO **ew**, **or**, AND **ir** SAY?

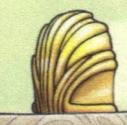

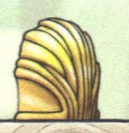

Learn:

- Write and say the sounds for multi-letter phonograms **ew**, **or**, and **ir**.
- Divide and read two-syllable words.

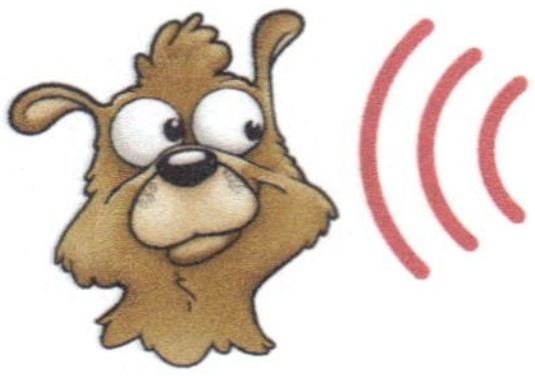

Listen and review.
Mark ☒ when done.

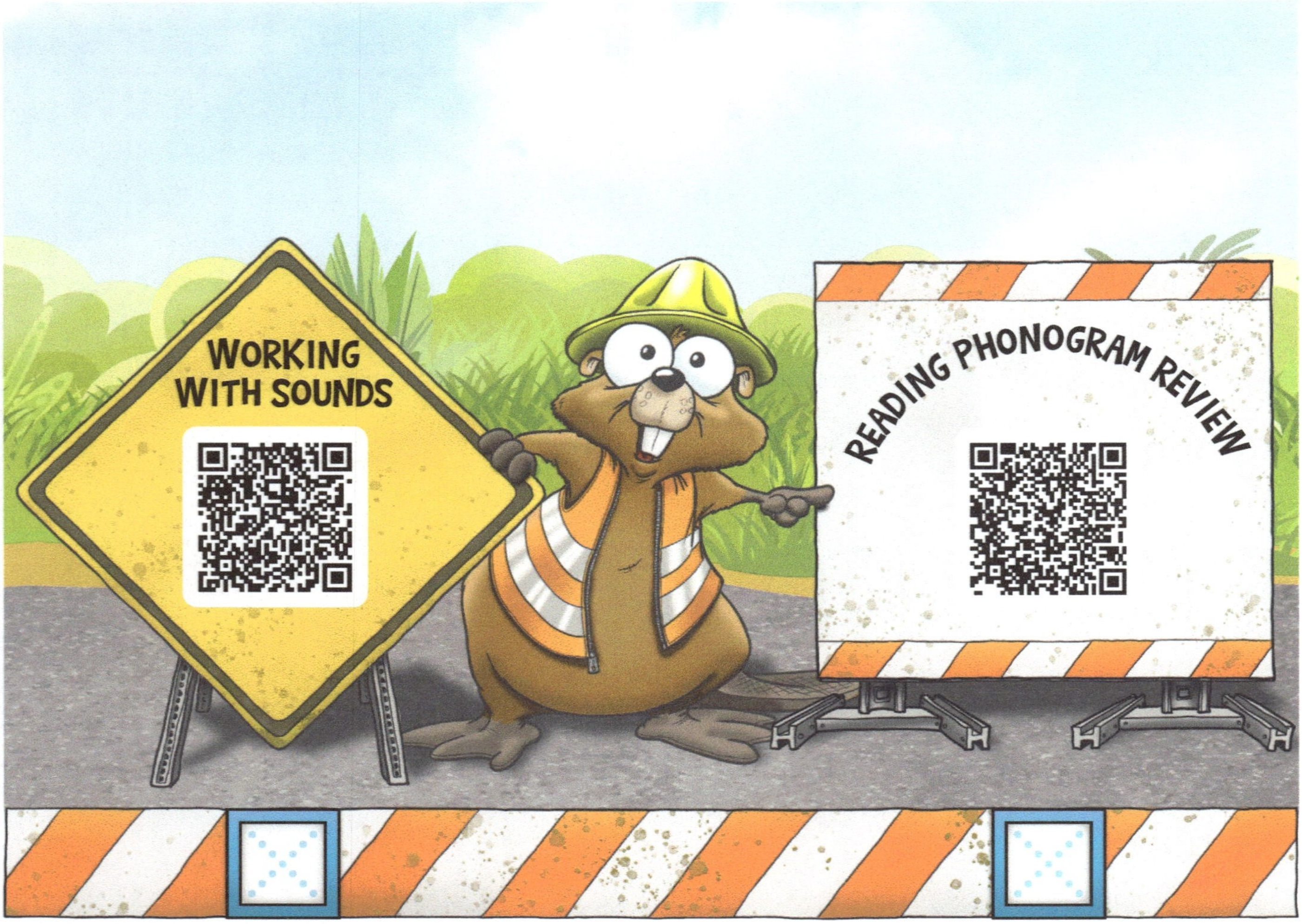
WORKING WITH SOUNDS
READING PHONOGRAM REVIEW

n**ew**   ch**ew**

Write and say the sound.
Underline the multi-letter phonograms.

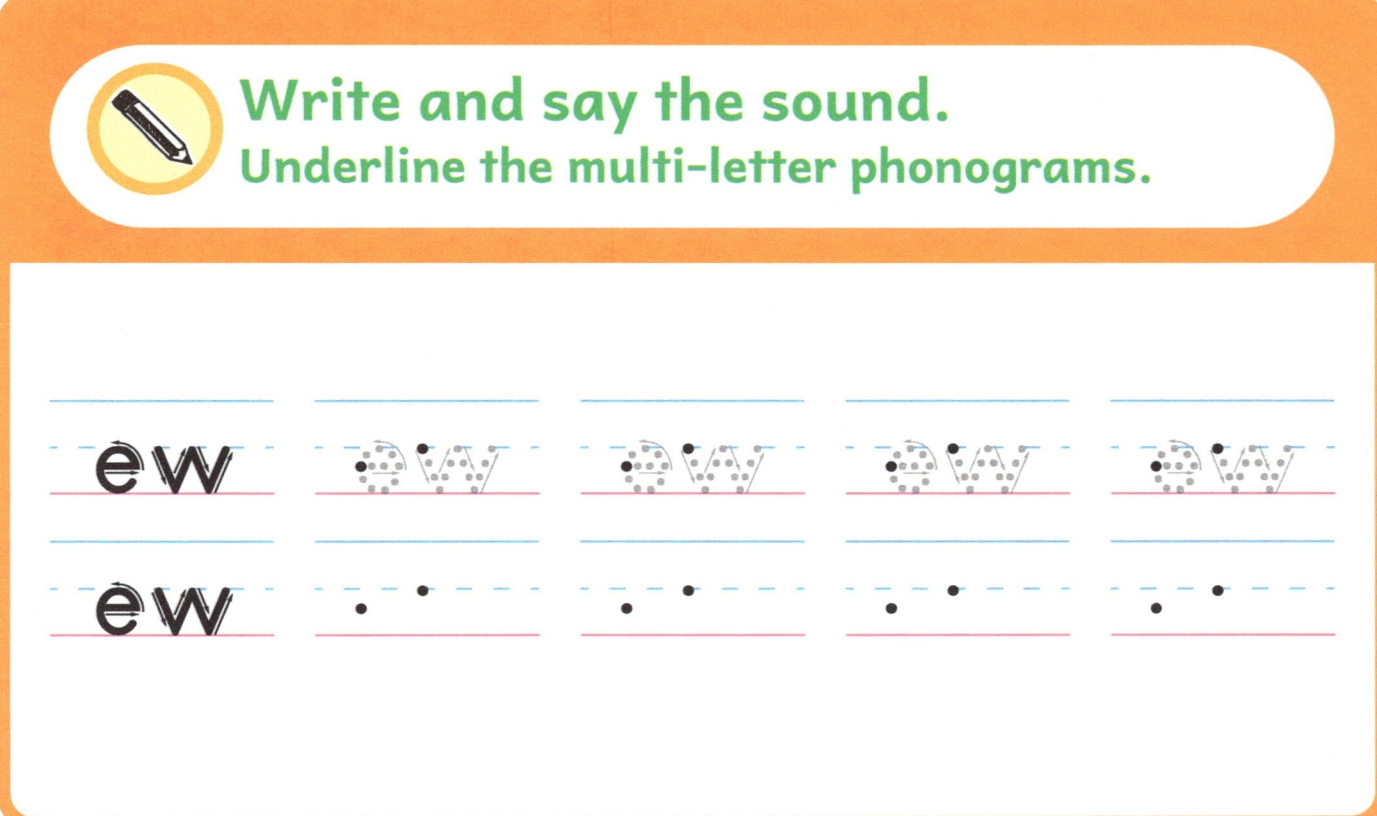

h**or**se   sp**or**t

✏️ Write and say the sound.
Underline the multi-letter phonograms.

or   or   or   or   or

or

54

th**ir**d   g**ir**l

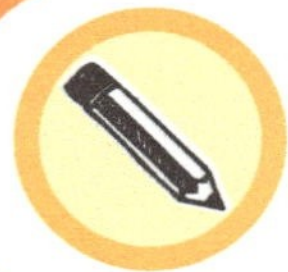

ir   ir   ir   ir   ir

ir

55

 **Read and write the words.**

shirt	stew	threw

1)

2)

3)

fork	corn	bird

4)

5)

6)

56

Reading Rules

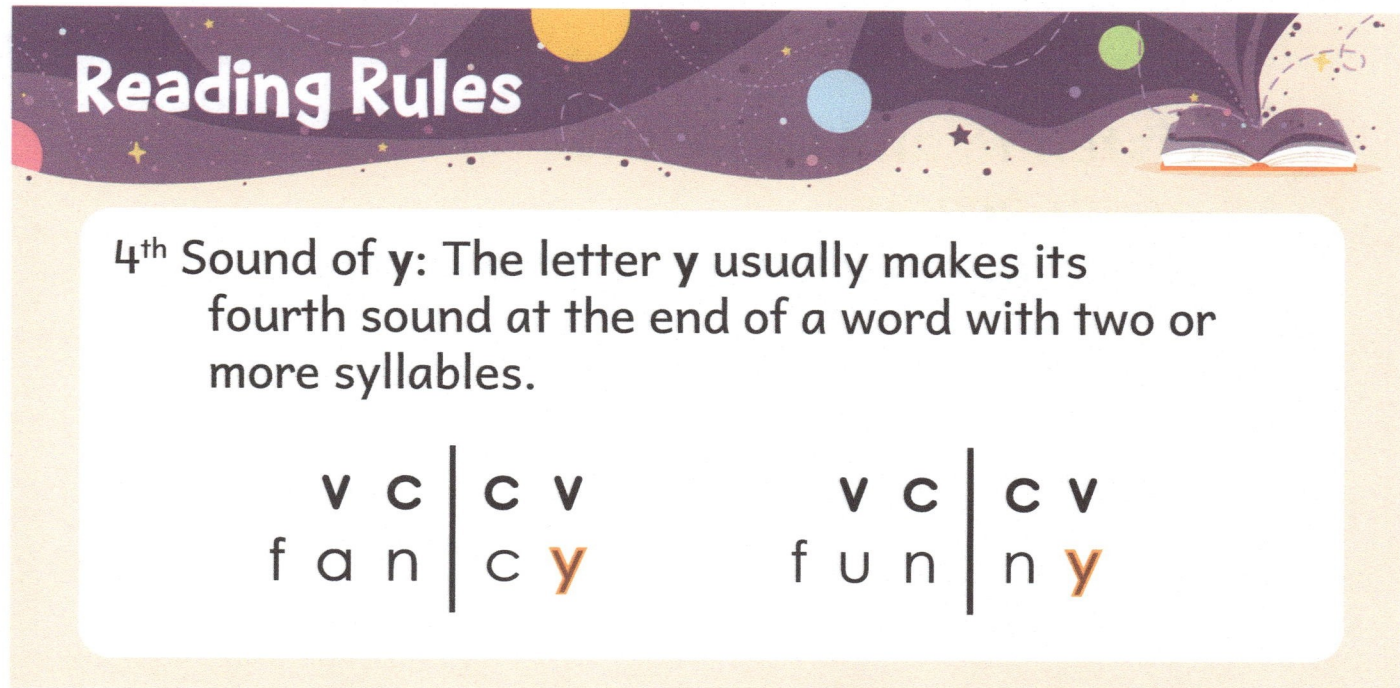

4th Sound of **y**: The letter **y** usually makes its fourth sound at the end of a word with two or more syllables.

v	c		c	v
f	a	n	c	**y**

v	c		c	v
f	u	n	n	**y**

 **Mark, divide, and read the VCCV words.**

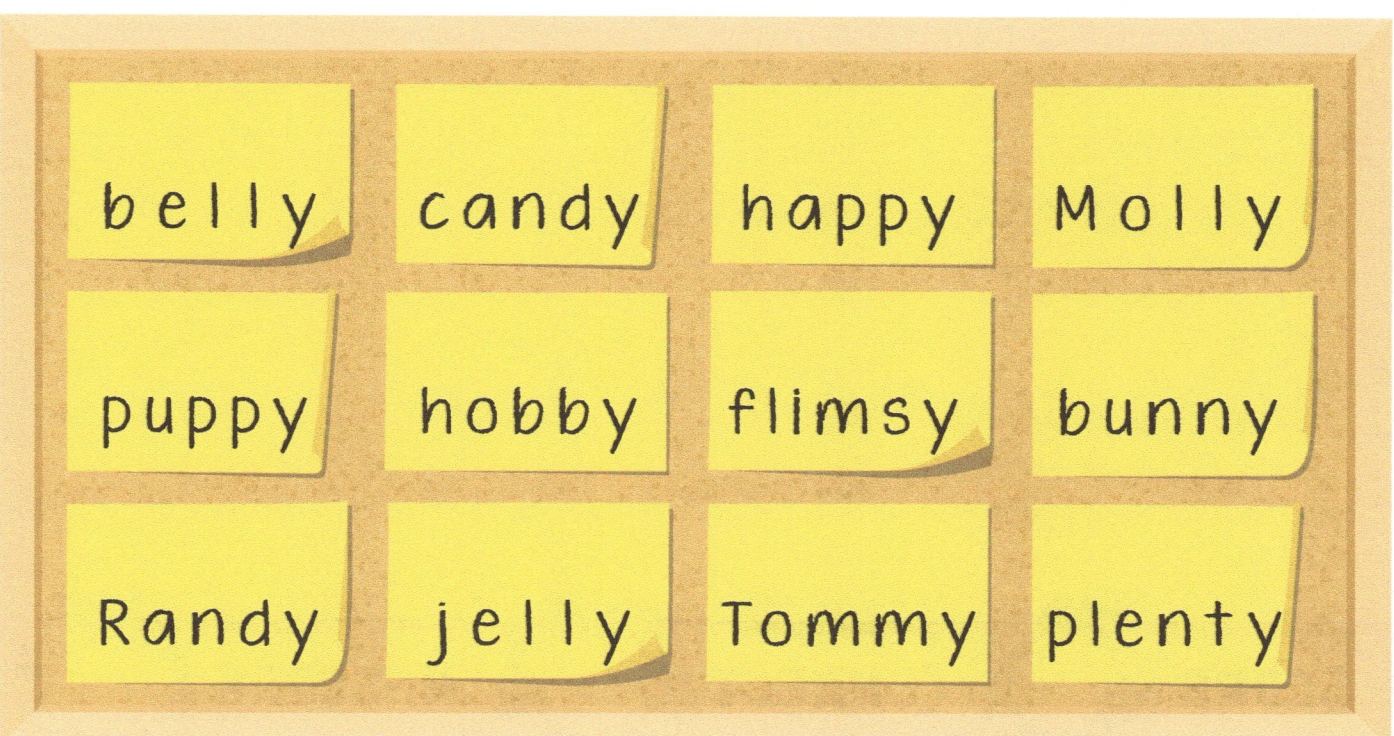

belly   candy   happy   Molly

puppy   hobby   flimsy   bunny

Randy   jelly   Tommy   plenty

WRITING PHONOGRAM REVIEW

Listen to and write the phonograms.
Underline any multi-letter phonograms.

SCORE   CORRECT   RESCORE

PHONOGRAM REVIEW

 Listen to and circle the correct phonograms.

1)    oy   oi   ou

2)    r   or   er

3)    c   ck   ch

4)    oy   oo   ow

5)    ch   k   ck

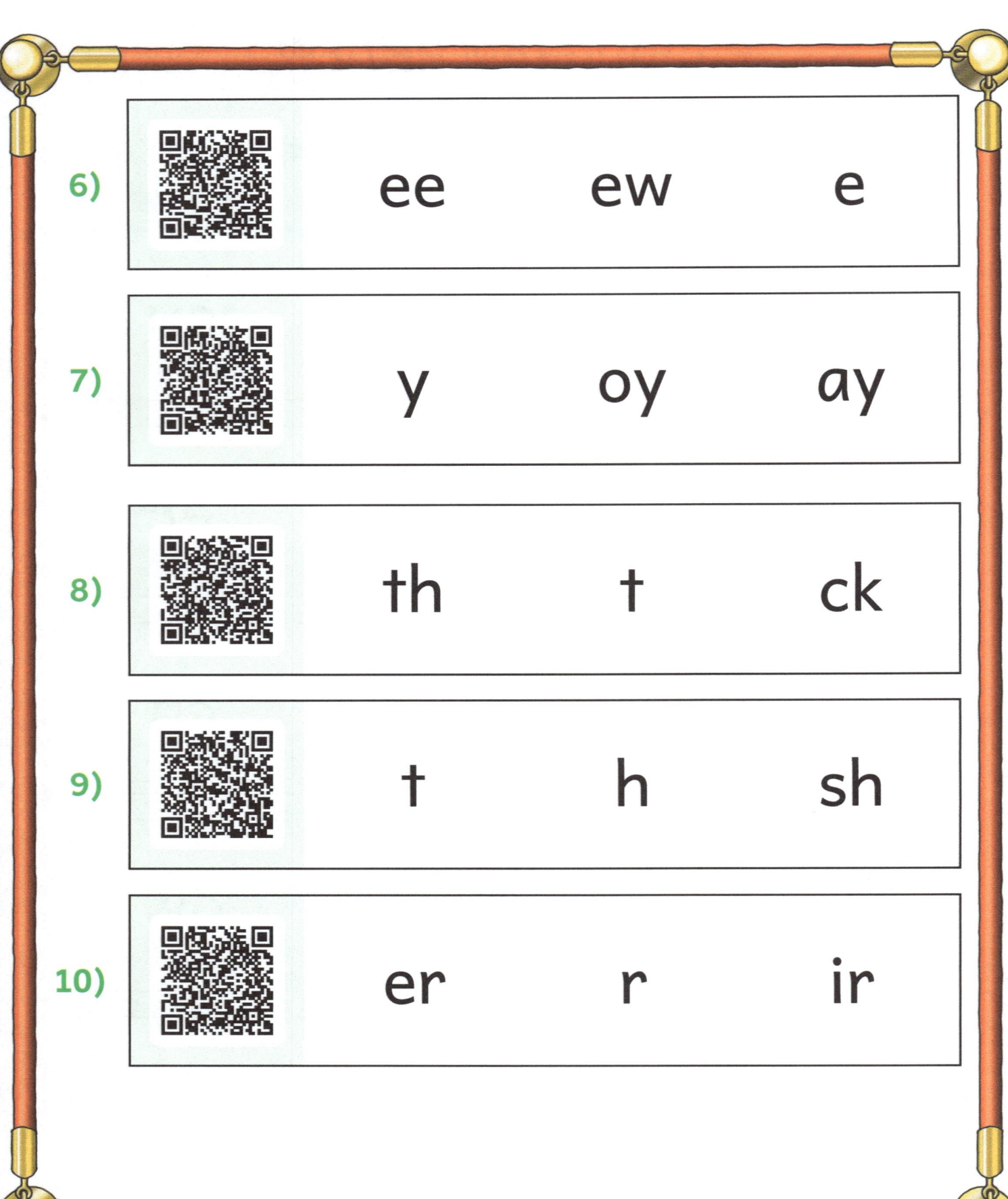

6) ee   ew   e

7) y   oy   ay

8) th   t   ck

9) t   h   sh

10) er   r   ir

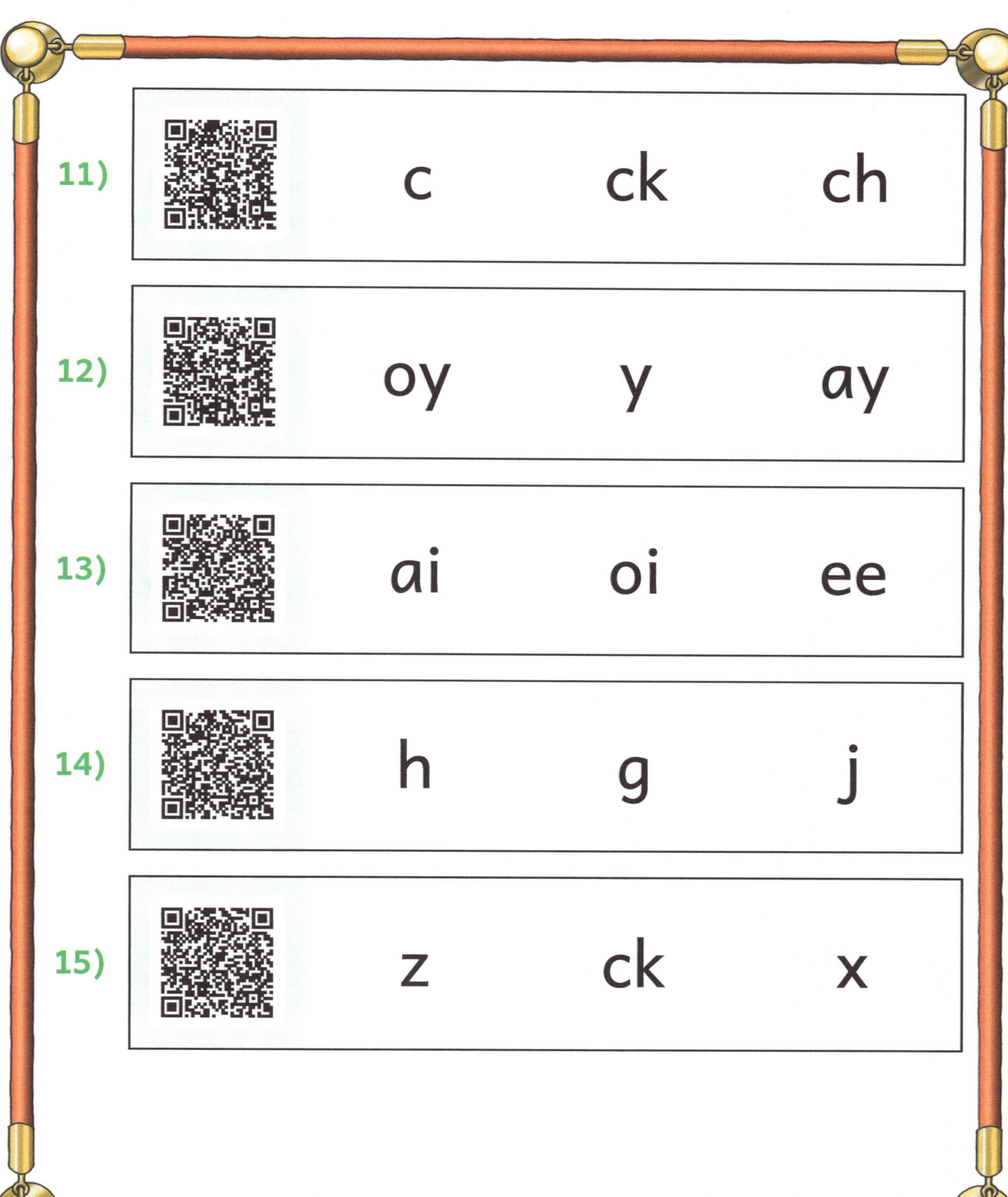

11) c   ck   ch

12) oy   y   ay

13) ai   oi   ee

14) h   g   j

15) z   ck   x

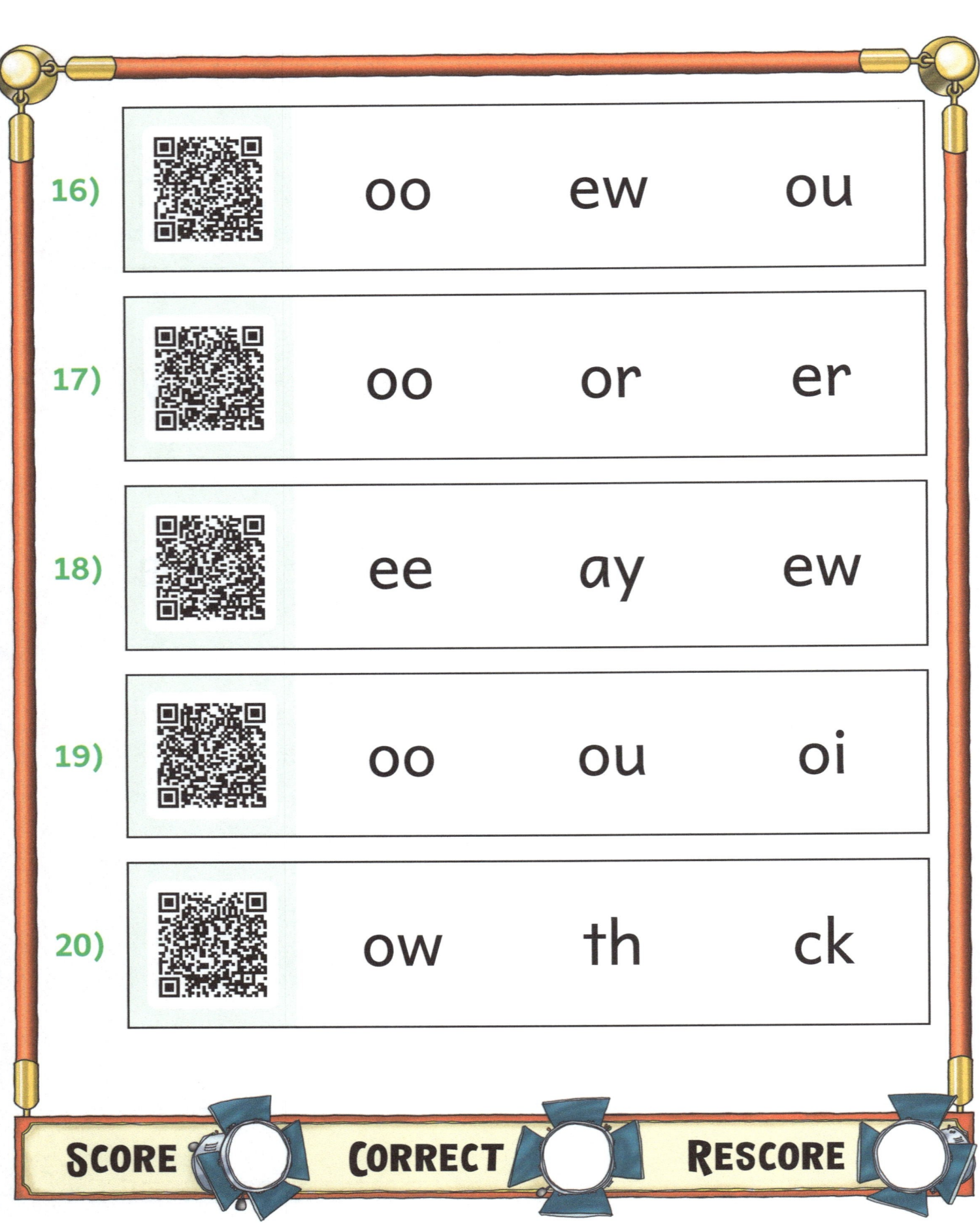

16)   oo   ew   ou

17)   oo   or   er

18)   ee   ay   ew

19)   oo   ou   oi

20)   ow   th   ck

SCORE   CORRECT   RESCORE

READER 3: "Quack Gets the Mail"

Practice these everyday words.

Read	Trace	Read	Trace
1) first	first	6) out	out
2) for	for	7) play	play
3) new	new	8) see	see
4) now	now	9) to	to
5) or	or	10) you	you

Time to Read!

Reader 3

Quack Gets the Mail

 **Choose the correct answers.**

11) What was in Kit's bowl?
- ○ stew
- ○ clay
- ○ mail

12) What was in the sack?
- ○ stew
- ○ clay
- ○ mail

13) What does Quack do?
- ○ make the stew
- ○ play with clay
- ○ sort the mail

14) Do the words *Bab* and *crab* end with the same sound?
- ○ yes
- ○ no

Phonogram Test 8

Listen to and write the correct phonograms.
Underline any multi-letter phonograms.

1)

2)

3)

4)

5)

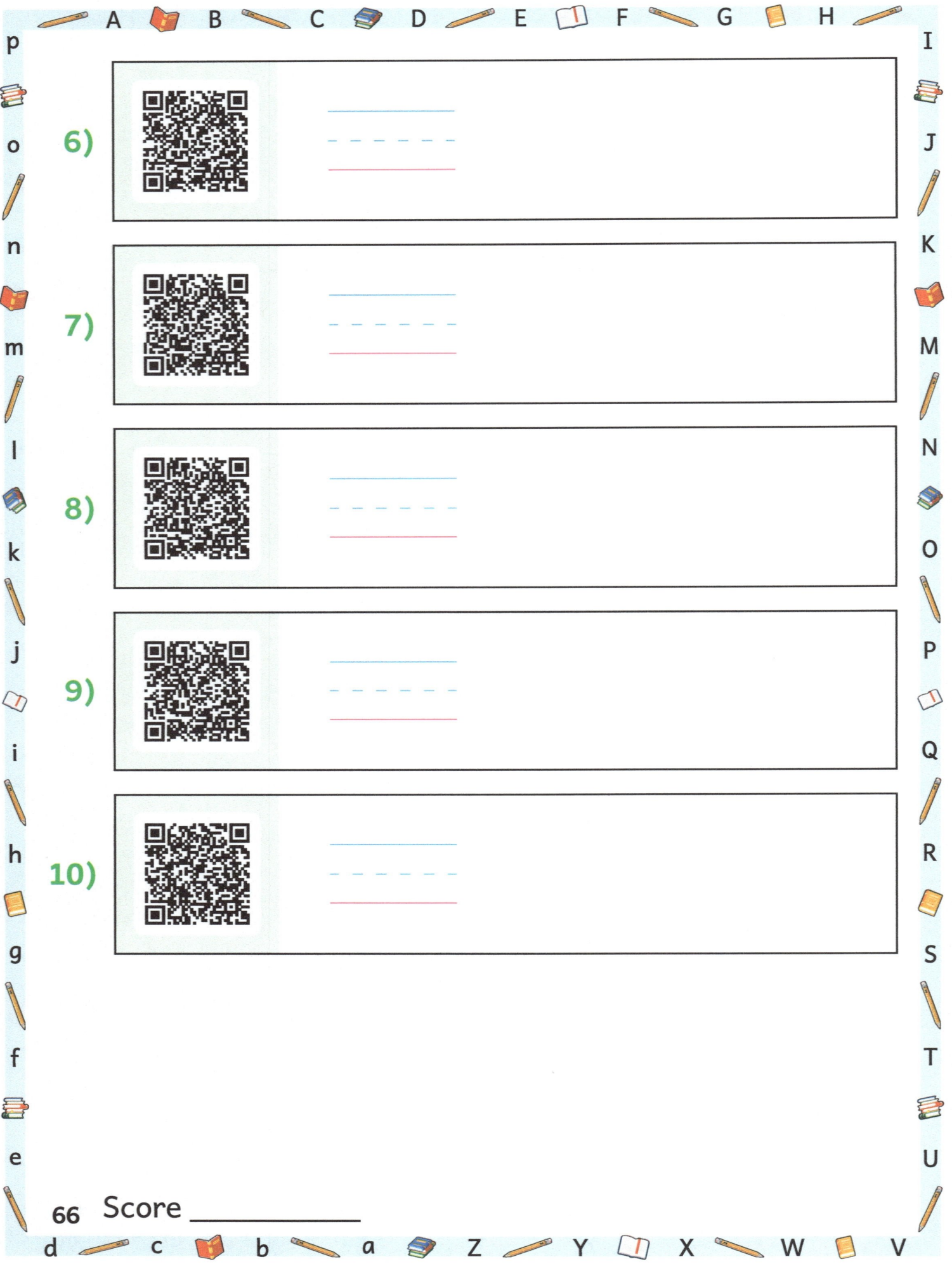

Score _____

7. WHAT DO **ar** AND **ur** SAY?

Learn:

- Write and say the sounds for multi-letter phonograms **ar** and **ur**.

- Divide and read two-syllable words.

Listen and review.
Mark ☒ when done.

p**ar**ty c**ar**d

✏️ **Write and say the sound.**
Underline the multi-letter phonograms.

ar   ar   ar   ar   ar

ar   .   .   .   .

t**ur**bo   s**ur**f

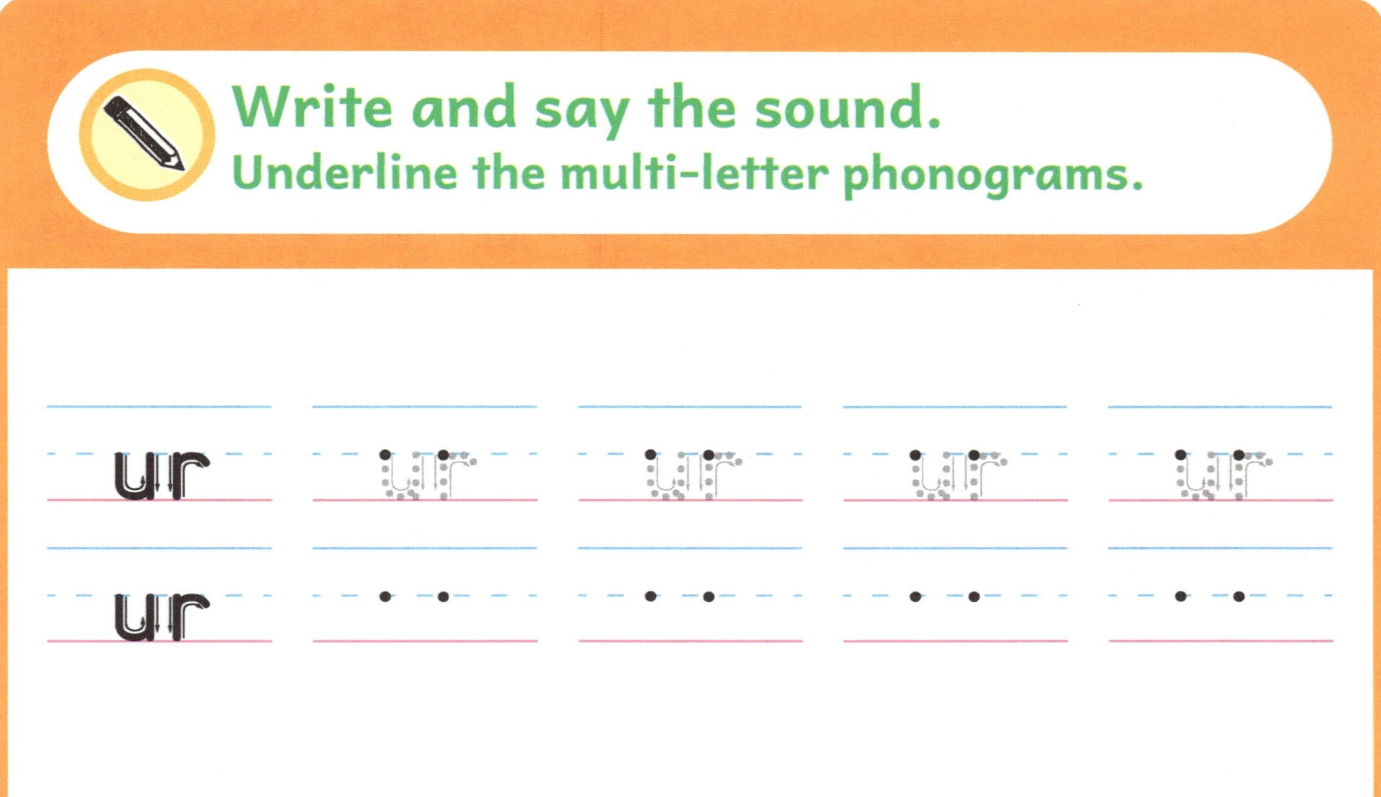

✏️ **Write and say the sound.**
Underline the multi-letter phonograms.

ur   ur   ur   ur   ur

ur

 **Read and write the words.**

farm	star	car

1)

2)

3)

fur	slurp	curl

4)

5)

6)

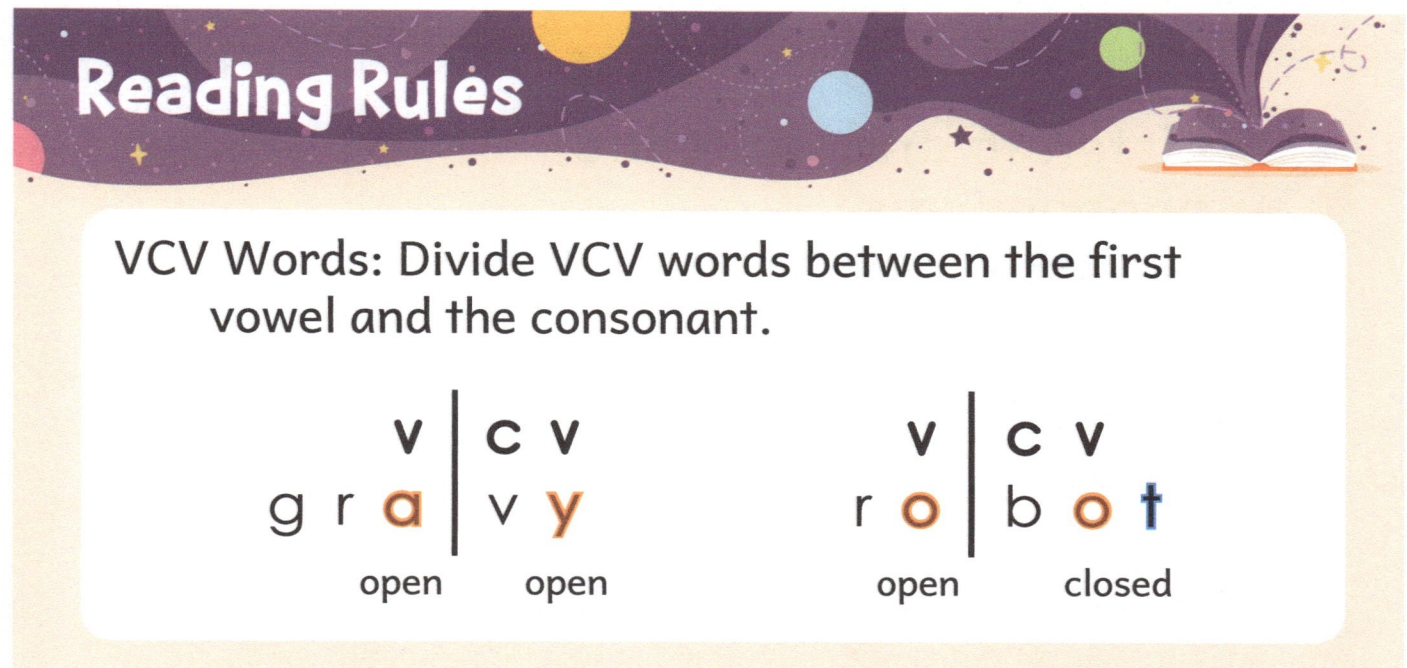

Reading Rules

VCV Words: Divide VCV words between the first vowel and the consonant.

v | c v
gr **a** | v **y**
open   open

v | c v
r **o** | b **o** t
open   closed

 **Mark, divide, and read the VCV words.**

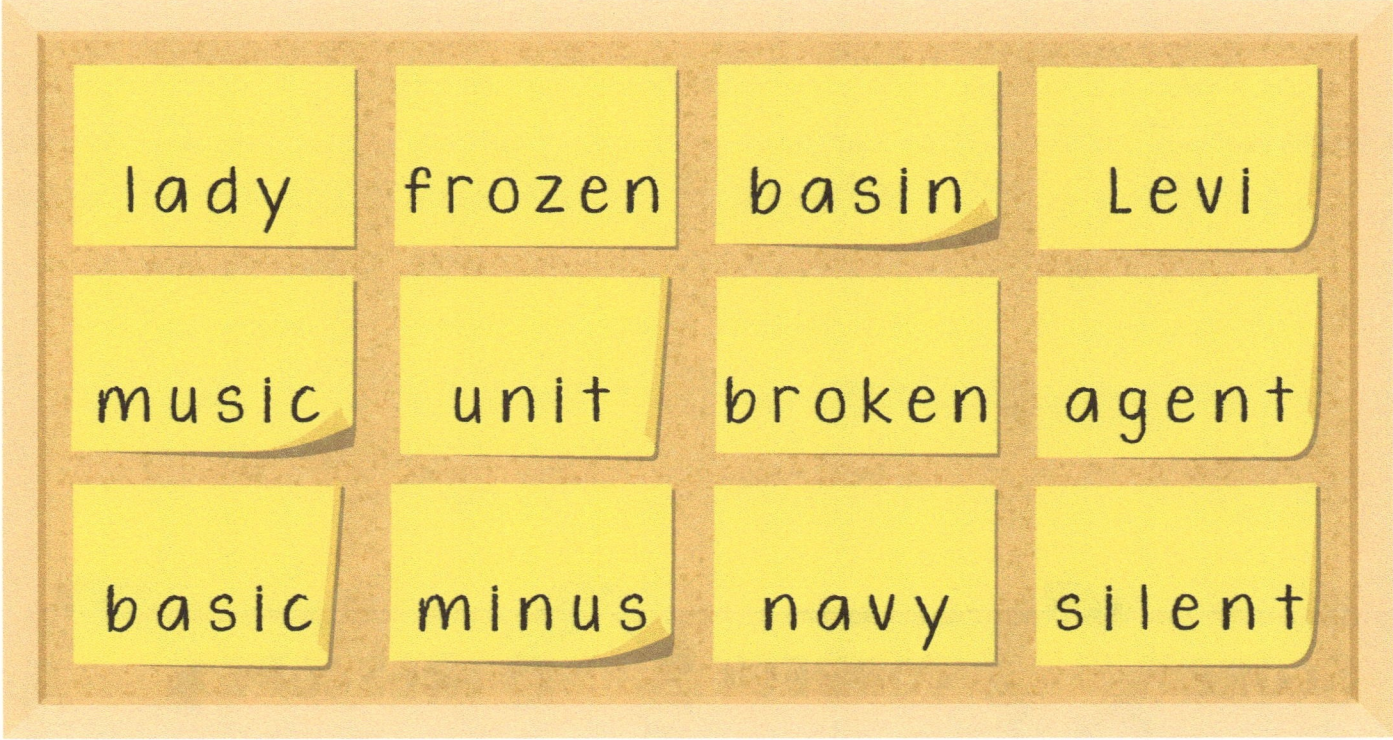

lady	frozen	basin	Levi
music	unit	broken	agent
basic	minus	navy	silent

WRITING PHONOGRAM REVIEW

 **Listen to and write the phonograms.**
Underline any multi-letter phonograms.

SCORE   CORRECT   RESCORE

8. WHAT DO **ng** AND **nk** SAY?

Learn:

- Write and say the sounds for multi-letter phonograms **ng** and **nk**.

- Divide and read two-syllable words.

Listen and review.
Mark ☒ when done.

ng

lo**ng** wi**ng**

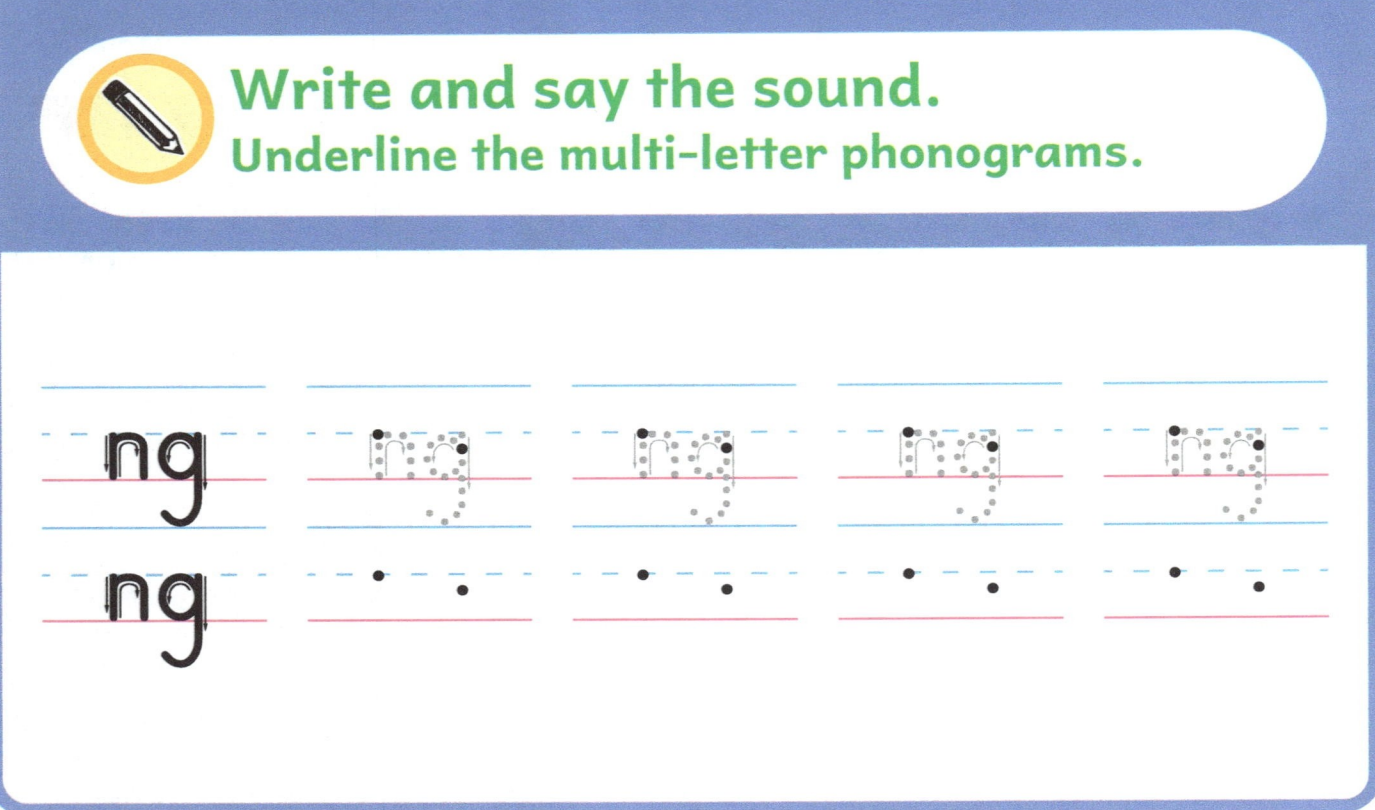

Write and say the sound.
Underline the multi-letter phonograms.

ng

ng

sku**nk**   stu**nk**

Write and say the sound.
Underline the multi-letter phonograms.

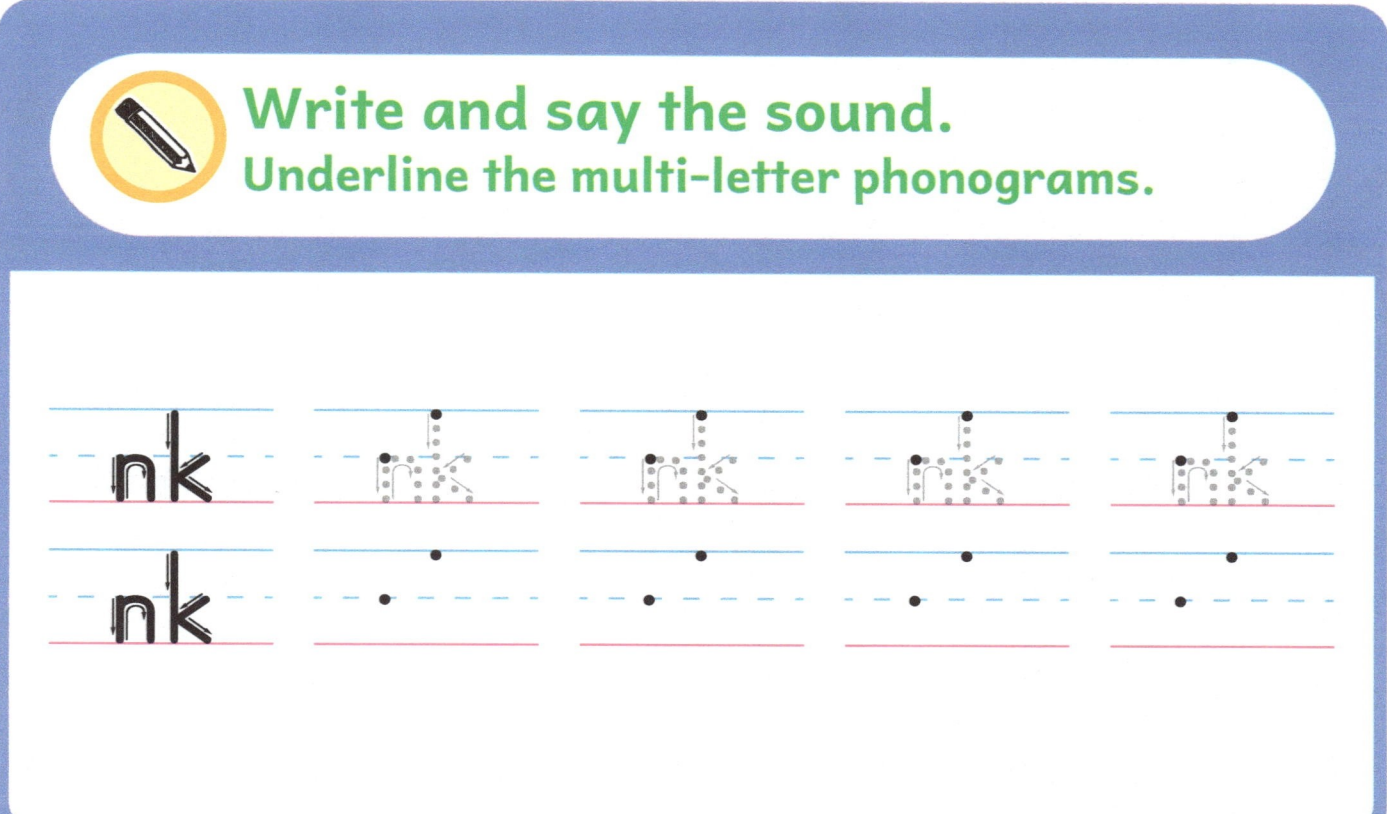

nk

nk

75

 **Read and write the words.**

song strong ring

1)

2)

3)

_____

trunk wink tank

4)

5)

6)

_____

WORKING WITH WORDS

Reading Rules

We will keep working with VCV words.

v	c	v		v	c	v
l **o**	g	**o**		**i**	t	**e** **m**
open		open		open		closed

 **Mark, divide, and read the VCV words.**

solo   David   topaz   raven

focus   cozy   pony   hotel

even   baby   omit   Venus

WRITING PHONOGRAM REVIEW

Listen to and write the phonograms.
Underline any multi-letter phonograms.

SCORE   CORRECT   RESCORE

ACTIVITY: Everyday Words

Read, trace, and write the words.

Read	Trace	Write
far	far	
for	for	
first	first	
new	new	
long	long	
thing	thing	
think	think	
now	now	
our	our	
look	look	

9. WHAT DO **aw**, **au**, AND **wh** SAY?

Learn:

- Write and say the sounds for multi-letter phonograms **aw**, **au**, and **wh**.

- Divide and read two-syllable words.

Listen and review.
Mark ☒ when done.

str**aw** l**aw**n

Write and say the sound.
Underline the multi-letter phonograms.

aw

aw

s**au**sage   s**au**ce

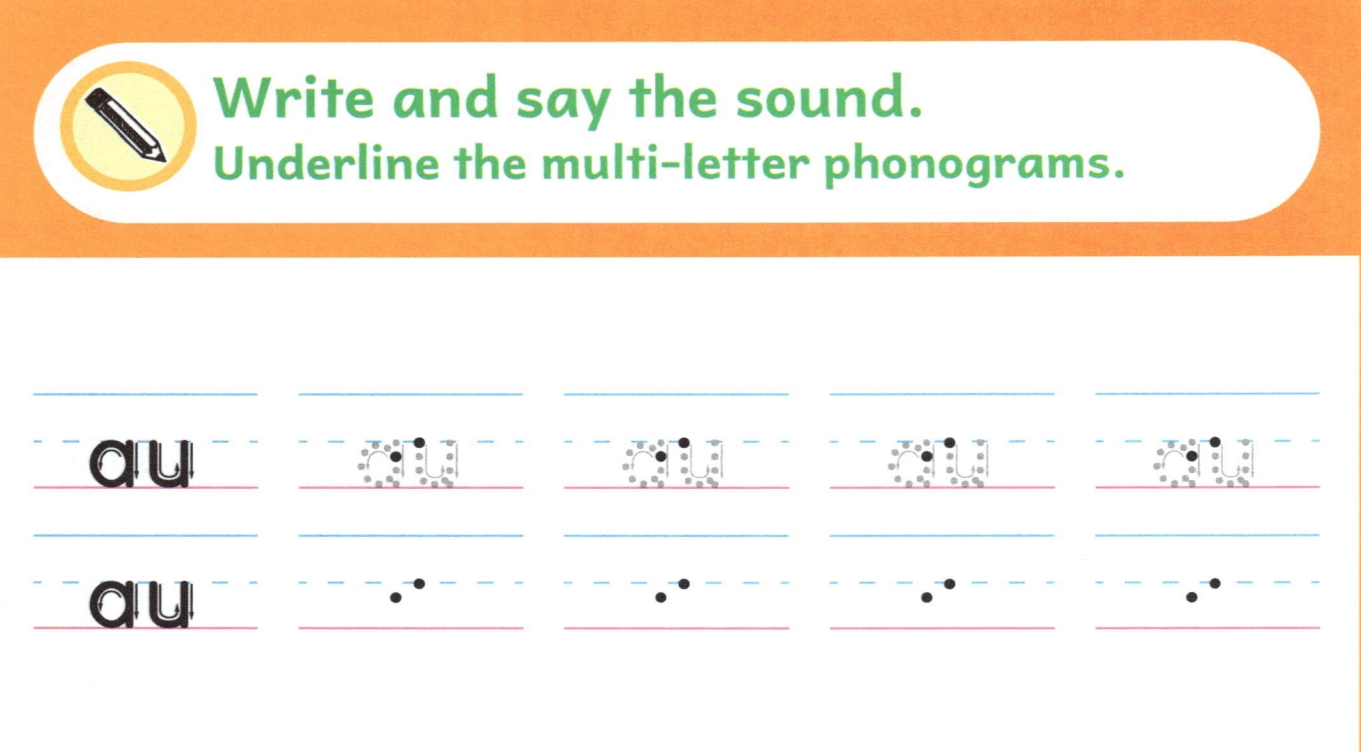

Write and say the sound.
Underline the multi-letter phonograms.

au   au   au   au   au

au   au   au   au   au

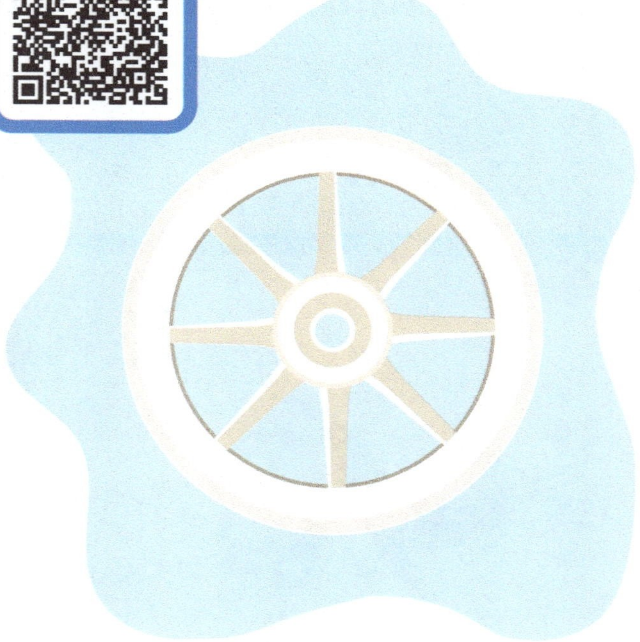

white **wh**eel

✏️ Write and say the sound.
Underline the multi-letter phonograms.

wh wh wh wh wh

wh

 **Read and write the words.**

paw	whale	yawn

1)

2)

3)

whisk	launch	aunt

4)

5)

6)

84

WORKING WITH WORDS

Reading Rules

Suffix **s** after VCe Words: When suffix **s** is added to a VCe word that ends with a sound of **j**, **s**, or **z**, the silent final **e** makes a short **e** sound. The first vowel sound is still long.

The VCV pattern can help you read these words.

	V	C	V	
r	o	s	e	s
	open	closed		

	V	C	V	
p	a	g	e	s
	open	closed		

Mark, divide, and read the VCV words.

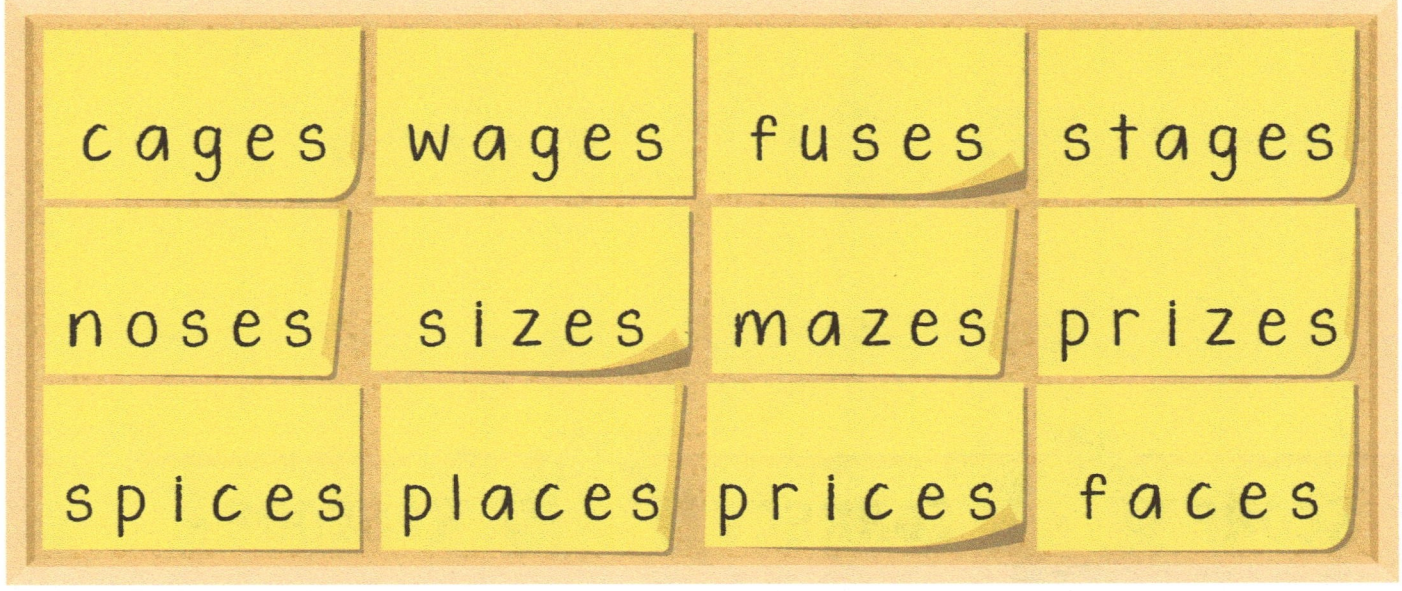

cages	wages	fuses	stages
noses	sizes	mazes	prizes
spices	places	prices	faces

 **Listen to and write the phonograms.**
Underline any multi-letter phonograms.

PHONOGRAM REVIEW

? **Listen to and circle the correct phonograms.**

1) 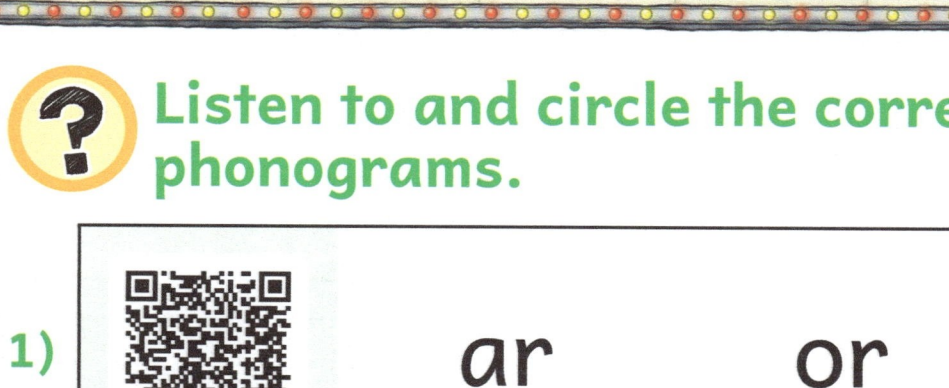 ar   or   er

2) sh   wh   nk

3) ay   ou   au

4) ck   ch   nk

5) a   ai   ay

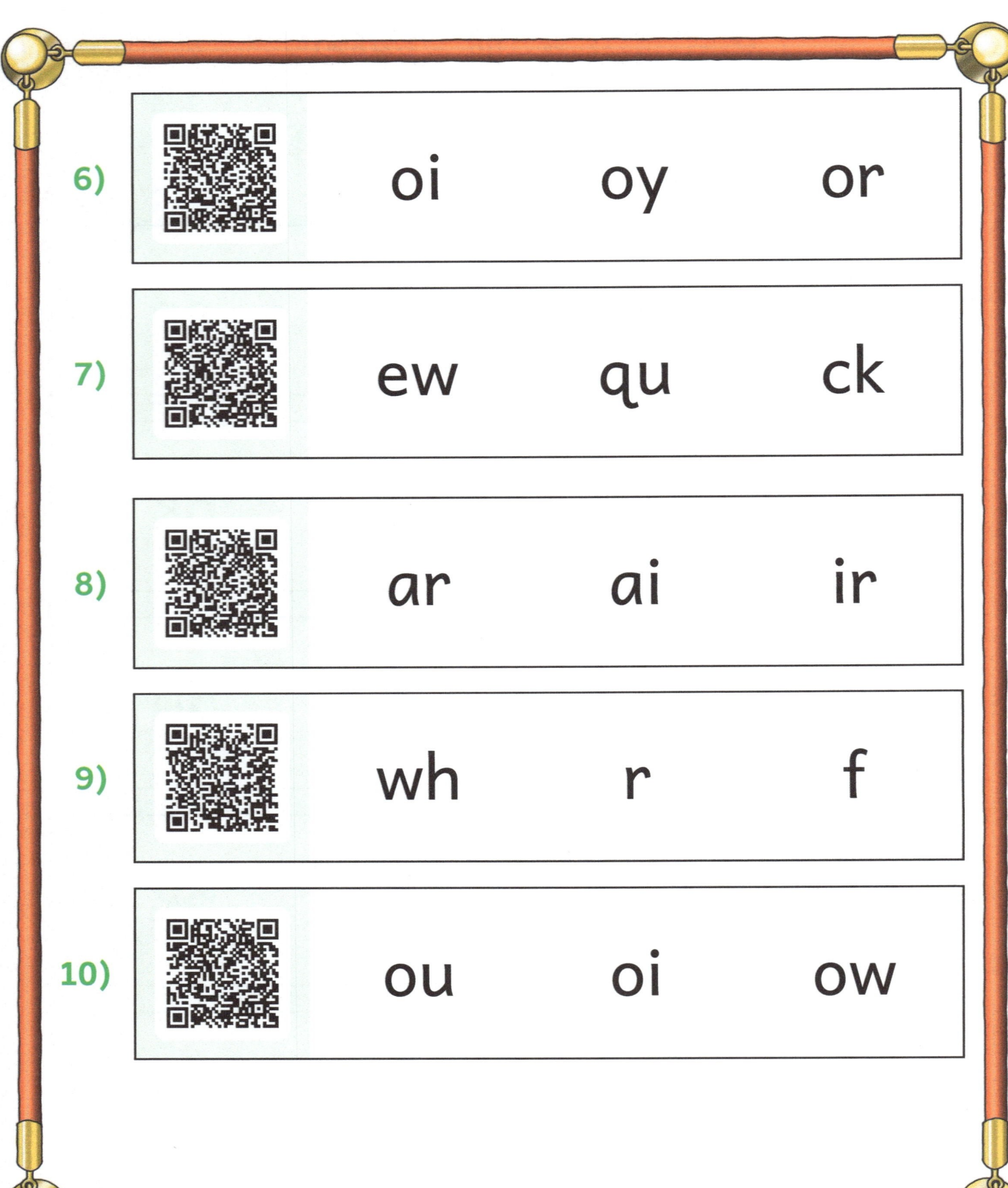

6)   oi   oy   or

7)   ew   qu   ck

8)   ar   ai   ir

9)   wh   r   f

10)   ou   oi   ow

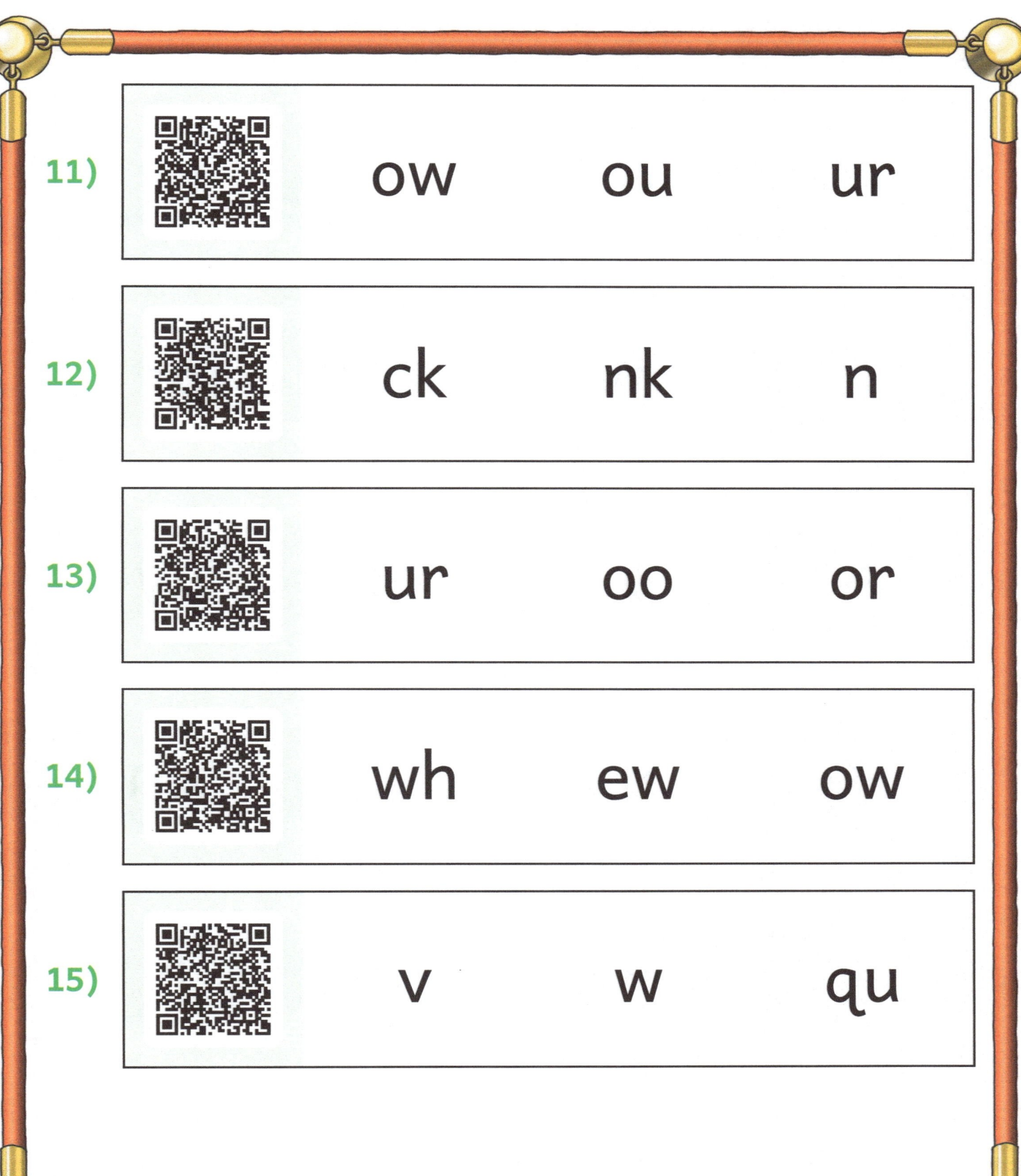

11) ow   ou   ur

12) ck   nk   n

13) ur   oo   or

14) wh   ew   ow

15) v   w   qu

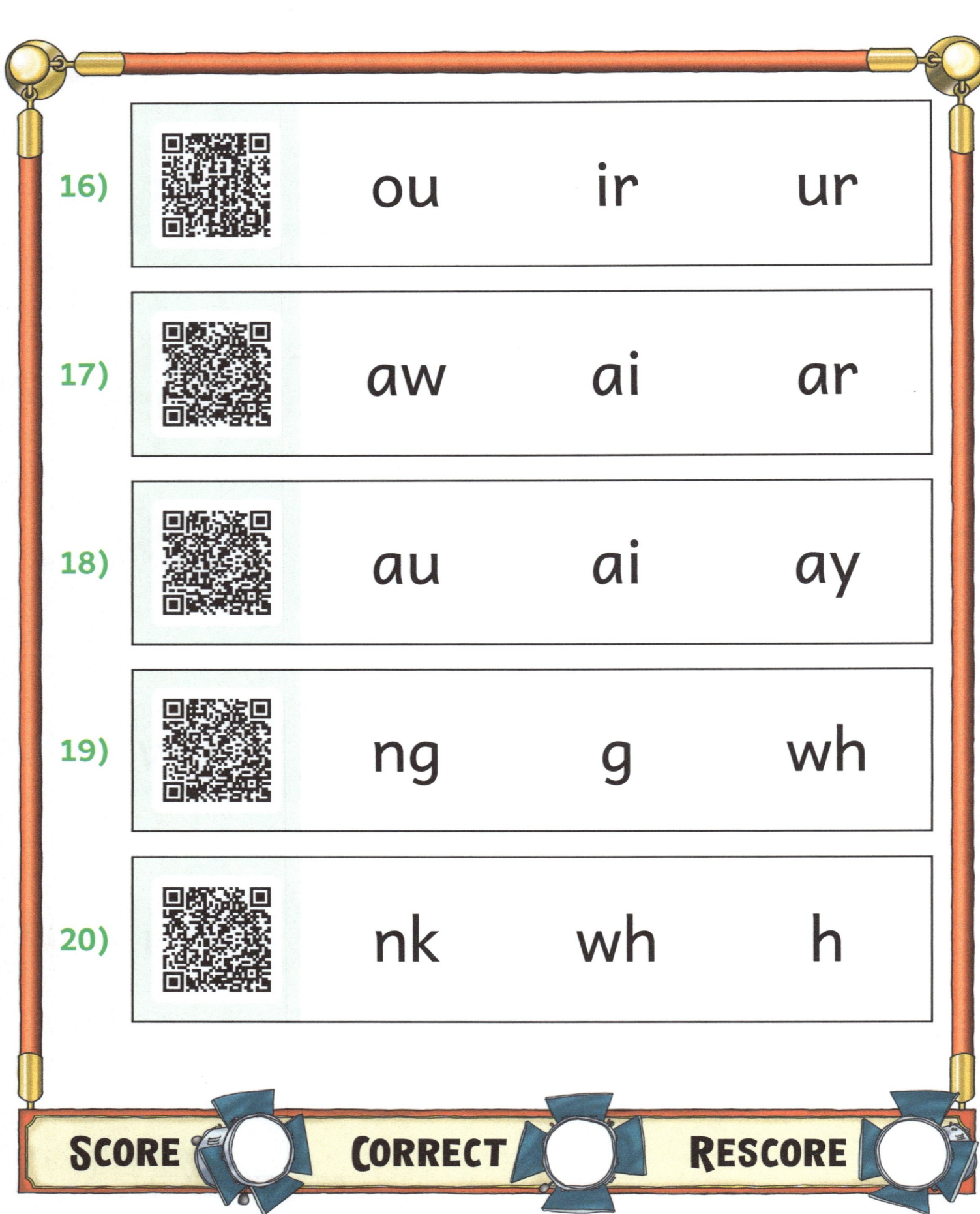

16)   ou   ir   ur

17)   aw   ai   ar

18)   au   ai   ay

19)   ng   g   wh

20)   nk   wh   h

SCORE   CORRECT   RESCORE

READER 4: "What Can Pip Do?"

Practice these everyday words.

Read	Trace		Read	Trace
1) and	and	6) think	think
2) do	do	7) what	what
3) good	good	8) with	with
4) her	her	9) you	you
5) the	the	10) is	is

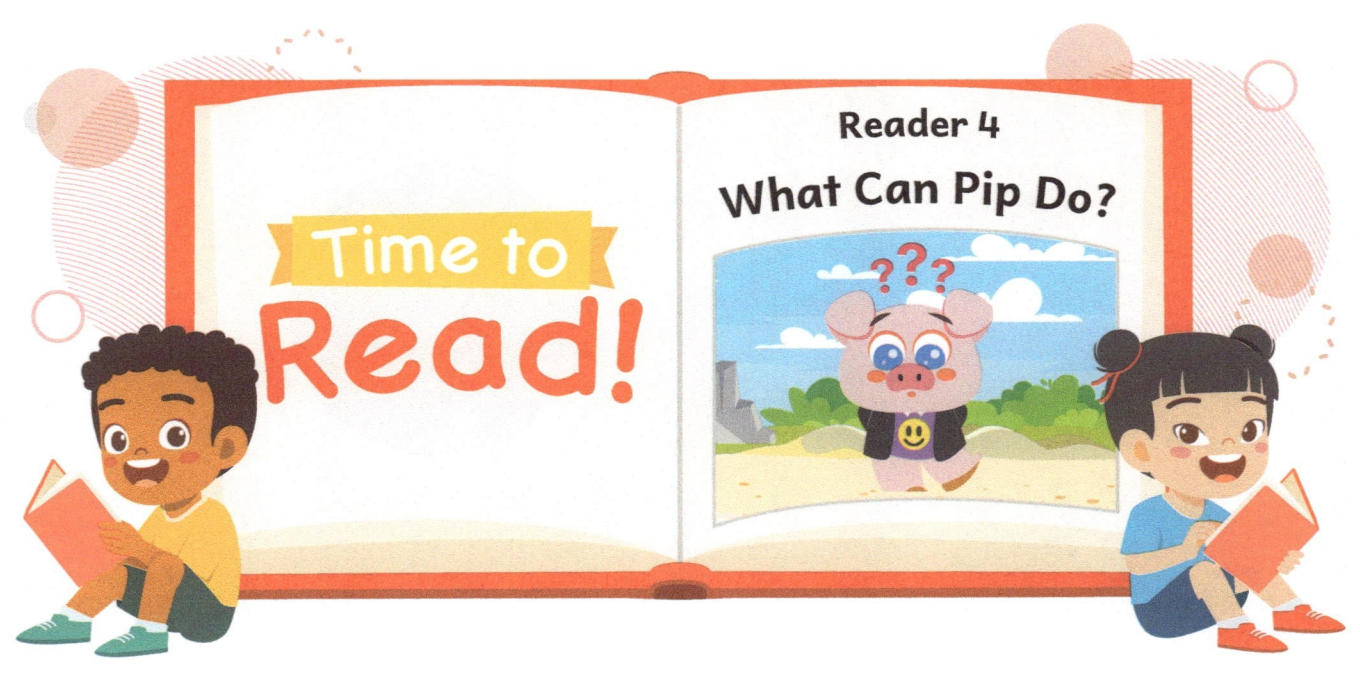

Time to Read!

Reader 4

What Can Pip Do?

 **Choose the correct answers.**

11) Who is good with art?
- ○ Quack
- ○ Zip
- ○ Bix

12) Mark ⊠ TWO things Quack can do.
- ☐ sing a song
- ☐ surf on the turf
- ☐ haul the mail

Write the correct answer.

13) What is one thing Pip can do?

Phonogram Test 9

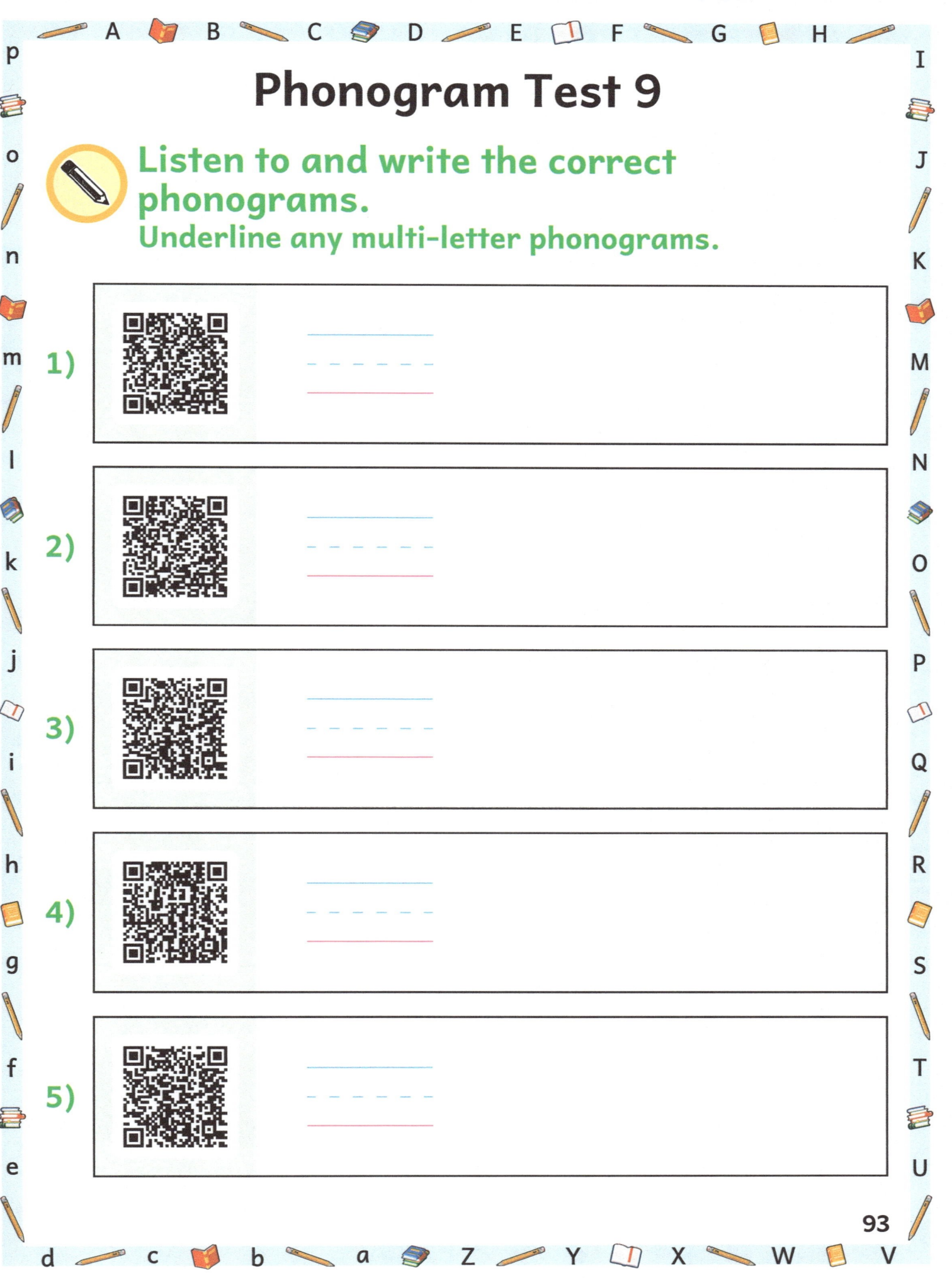

✏️ **Listen to and write the correct phonograms.**
Underline any multi-letter phonograms.

1)

2)

3)

4)

5)

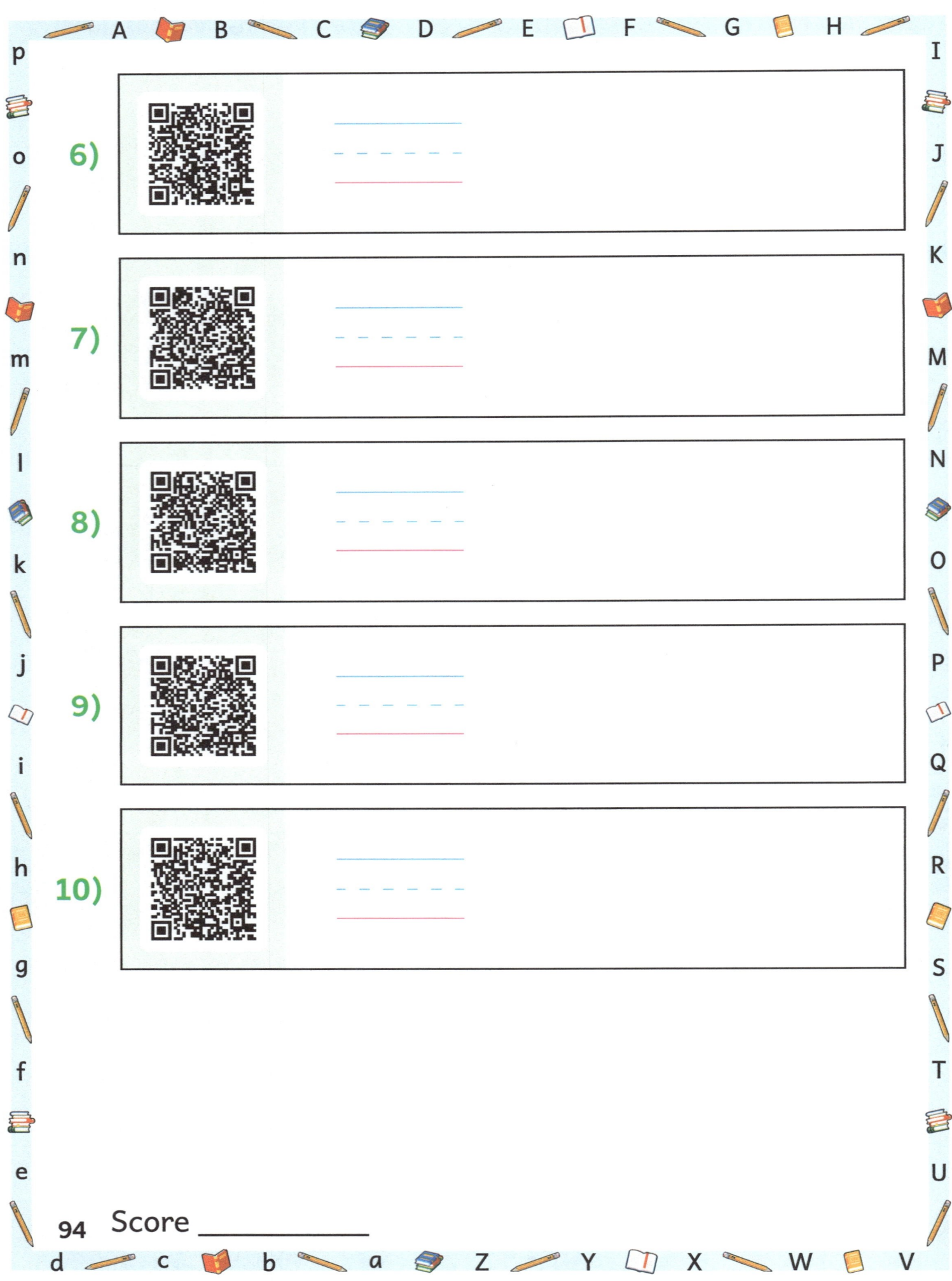

6)

7)

8)

9)

10)

Score _____